OPPORTUNITIES

in

W9-BZA-618

Marketing
Careers

REVISED EDITION

MARGERY STEINBERG

McGraw·Hill

New York   Chicago   San Francisco   Lisbon   London   Madrid   Mexico City
Milan   New Delhi   San Juan   Seoul   Singapore   Sydney   Toronto

To Lew

1 2 3 4 5 6 7 8 9 0   DOC/DOC   0 9 8 7 6 5

ISBN 0-07-144898-5

Interior design by Rattray Design

McGraw-Hill books are available at special quantity discounts to use as premiums and sales promotions, or for use in corporate training programs. For more information, please write to the Director of Special Sales, Professional Publishing, McGraw-Hill, Two Penn Plaza, New York, NY 10121-2298. Or contact your local bookstore.

This book is printed on acid-free paper.

Contents

(industrial) marketing. Marketing education. Consulting.

Foreword

Among the many careers in business—accounting, finance, manufacturing, purchasing, personnel, and so on—marketing is one of the most exciting and rewarding. "There is never a dull moment" certainly applies to this field. Talk to people in sales, advertising, product planning, sales promotion, and marketing research, and they will tell you that each day brings new challenges and calls for new solutions.

Marketing people get involved in one of two tasks. One task is to identify unsatisfied consumer needs and wants that might provide promising new business opportunities. Thus the Ford marketing people discovered many years ago that many young people would like to buy an affordable sports car—and they launched the Mustang. Identifying new opportunities involves market researchers, product developers, pricing experts, and market planners.

The second task is to attract new customers to existing products, services, and brands. This calls for identifying the groups of people who would benefit most from an offer, preparing advertising to communicate the offer's benefits, making sales calls on prospects, designing sales promotions to stimulate purchase, negotiating, and several other skills.

Marketing is not only a challenge to business firms that produce products and services but also to government agencies and non-profit organizations as well. Thus the U.S. Post Office is now competing with many private carriers of the mail such as Federal Express for mail business. And theater groups, social service agencies, colleges, and hospitals have turned to marketing to attract customers and raise more donor money.

I have worked in the marketing field for more than thirty years—as a teacher, writer, consultant, and trainer—and I find continuous challenge in the new problems and issues that arise, whether it is the Chrysler Corporation trying to figure out how to compete more effectively, Apple Computer considering whether it should launch a new computer model, or McDonald's deciding whether to introduce a new food product. You will gain the same enthusiasm for marketing as you read Margery Steinberg's excellent discussion on careers in marketing.

Philip Kotler
Northwestern University

Preface

THE INTERNET, ESPECIALLY that portion known as the World Wide Web, has the potential to change radically the way businesses interact with their customers. The Web frees customers from their traditionally passive role as receivers of marketing communications, gives them much greater control over the information search and acquisition process, and allows them to become active participants in the marketing process.*

How would you like to become part of one of the most in demand and increasingly important areas of career opportunity? Do you want to prepare for a job that is challenging, creative, and holds the promise of high personal and professional growth? If so read on, for no matter what career you choose, what business you select, or what company you work for, marketing will play a more and more prominent role in your life. Not only has

---

* Hoffman, Donna, Thomas Novak, and Patrali Chattergee, "Commercial Scenarios for the Web: Opportunities and Challenges," *Journal of Computer Mediated Communications* 1, no. 3 (December 1995).

the field grown enormously in the last few years, owing to new developments in understanding of the process, but organizations have placed a greater emphasis on the marketing function in response to our highly competitive environment as well. The field of marketing offers a dynamic, challenging, creative, and stimulating career. It also has its share of frustration and routine, but the energy level is such that the excitement usually wins out.

I hope to be able to convey some of that excitement to you as you read this book. Leaf through and glance at the career areas that interest you most, then look at some of the others for comparison. The chapter on education is focused primarily on the undergraduate level, but I have included information on advanced degrees as well.

Whether you are in high school and contemplating your future for the first time, employed and considering a career change, or already in the field and seeking advancement, I want you to gain some insight into a profession that is one of the fastest growing today.

You, the reader, will have to accept an active role in the planning and execution of your career, from the moment you first consider the prospect, through college or other preparation, and throughout every position you hold until retirement. A career is an ongoing, real job. Because you will spend most of your adult life involved in your career, it is to your benefit to take the time now to learn not only the basic skills needed but also to find out what type of work suits you best and what fields offer the greatest opportunities for self-fulfillment. Not only will you be happier in a career that you like, but people who like their work tend to do better in their jobs and thus are more likely to advance, increasing personal and professional growth, not to mention the financial rewards involved.

Give careful thought to your abilities—are you a people person or a lone ranger? While organizations require that certain skills be developed, such as the ability to work with others and be a team player, it is important to understand what your strengths are and how to use them to help you perform to the best of your ability.

It is not the purpose of this book to provide a rigid step-by-step program on how to become a marketer, but rather to present information about the field in a concise, useful manner to help you weigh the pros and cons against your own abilities and aspirations to reach a carefully considered career direction. Use this book as a tool, a source, a springboard for your individual research. Take the information presented here and apply it to yourself, your goals, and your dreams. You, and only you, can decide whether marketing is the right field for you. The best I can do is inform, which I attempt to do in the most complete and understandable way possible.

It is my hope that I can persuade some of you to join us in this dynamic field and accept the challenge marketing has to offer. Perhaps you will become a major force and make further contributions to the field. I hope so, and would like to think this book will play a role in that decision.

Margery Steinberg
Associate Professor of Marketing and Executive Director of
    The Center for Customer Service
University of Hartford

ACKNOWLEDGMENTS

WRITING A BOOK is not an easy task. Many minds and experiences contribute to an author's knowledge of the subject matter and understanding of the readers' needs and interests.

I hereby acknowledge those who contributed to this book: my colleagues at the University of Hartford, who have both challenged and supported me; my students, who have given me direction for my work through their curiosity about the field and their career interests; my research assistant Aanal Bhagat, who spent tireless hours on the Internet researching the most current and informative materials for this book; and former assistants Linda Plank, Roopa Majithia, and Sandor Erdei, who contributed greatly to the earlier editions of this book.

1

What Is Marketing All About?

Did you know that now you can buy products from a sewing needle to an Airbus aircraft sitting at home? Virtual grocery shopping is a reality for some consumers, who will soon experience the only online grocery service featuring full-motion video. This is possible due to e-marketing through virtual stores. These are examples of the result of good marketing.

Contrary to popular myths, marketers do not manipulate buyers, sell shoddy products, or make us buy things we don't need or want. Throughout this book you will learn about real marketing and, I hope, shed some of the misconceptions about the field.

Marketing Is a Dynamic and Exciting Field

A primary function of marketing is to educate customers about products and services. Persuading people to make informed purchase decisions is how marketing actually works.

To begin with, marketing in and of itself is nothing more than a powerful tool, and like any tool, in the wrong hands it can be misused. It is a means the marketing professional uses to analyze the market, understand customers, and present a product or service to the potential benefit of both buyer and seller. In other words, marketing is the bridge between product and customer. By itself marketing cannot force people to purchase an item they do not need or want (although some less-scrupulous persons might wish it could). What customers often see as the end result may be a reflection of society as it is or as we would like it to be. Don't forget that customers are the ones who ultimately decide—by voting with their purchase dollars—which products or services they want made available on the market.

The American Marketing Association (AMA), the international organization of marketing professionals, offers the following definition of marketing (www.marketingpower.com):

> Marketing is an organizational function and a set of processes for creating, communicating, and delivering value to customers and for managing customer relationships in ways that benefit the organization and its stakeholders.

We can expand this definition by noting that marketing is also "responding to the changing environment," that is, meeting the changing needs of customers. Marketing exists within the dynamic context of our social trends and cultural forces, and whatever is happening at the moment both domestically and globally. Understanding these activities and their effects—their impact on customers—is a goal of the marketing professional. One marketer I know likes to think there is really no magic to marketing, just that the practice of "applied common sense" works its own marvels.

Although marketing is thought of primarily in terms of promotional activity, this is just one of the four Ps of marketing: product, price, place, and promotion. These four building blocks, as identified by Philip Kotler, one of the foremost authors in the field, describe the basic functions of the marketing process. Not only is marketing more than selling and advertising, so are the careers in this field, such as research director, product manager, project supervisor, assistant buyer, and a whole host of others, which we will discuss later in the book.

As Ralph Waldo Emerson said, "Build a better mousetrap and the world will beat a path to your door." Product development and management are important pieces of marketing, and its ongoing process is based on listening to customers and responding to their needs.

How does the marketer learn what customers want? Marketing research is another major area of marketing, and surveys, questionnaires, and correspondence are statistically analyzed to yield customers' and potential customers' preferences and indicate trends. These and other areas of marketing will be discussed in detail in Chapter 2.

Encountering Marketing on a Day-to-Day Basis

Most people are more comfortable with the familiar   and marketing is really nothing exotic. See how marketing intertwines with your everyday life from the following examples:

- **Yourself.** From interviewing at a college or for a job to presentations in class, understanding the customer—the recipient of your message—will be vital to the success of your endeavor.
- **Your environment.** Proponents of political and social causes rely heavily on marketing techniques to ensure their message reaches and involves the greatest number of people who are potential supporters.

• **Your purchases (goods and services).** Every item you use is touched in some way by the four Ps: the product itself and its development from concept to concrete, its price and how it was determined, any promotional activity including word of mouth, and finally the place where it is sold and the distribution system that gets it there. Each time you call on a specialist in any field, whether plumber, physician, or pizza parlor, the marketing principle of the right product in the right place at the right time with the right price and the right promotion is employed. Think about it and you'll see how it all works together for you, the customer.

Marketing Careers

The following are brief descriptions of some of the basic types of jobs that marketers perform.

• **Marketing research professional.** This involves developing and administering questionnaires; collecting, coding, and tabulating data; analyzing the results; recommending applications and courses of action; gathering data on competitors and analyzing prices, sales, and methods of marketing and distribution; and designing telephone, mail, or Internet surveys to assess consumer preferences. Some surveys are conducted as personal interviews by going door-to-door, leading focus group discussions, or setting up booths in public places such as shopping malls. Trained interviewers, under the market research analyst's direction, usually conduct the surveys. They provide a company's management with information needed to make decisions on the promotion, distribution, design, and pricing of products or services.

• **Advertising professional.** The main functions of advertising are suggesting and developing the approach, creating the artwork, presenting ideas to the client, coordinating the production, recommending placement and securing the media space, providing the analysis of cost and reach, and coordinating with sales, marketing, and product management. There are new modes of marketing now such as on the Internet and through e-mail advertising.

• **Public relations professional.** The professionals involved in PR for marketing are in charge of monitoring the company name in periodicals and broadcasts, handling customer inquiries, organizing community or press events, writing ads, and releasing notices to the press. Public relations specialists handle organizational functions such as media, community, consumer, industry, and governmental relations; political campaigns; interest-group representation; conflict mediation; or employee and investor relations. They help an organization and its public adapt mutually to each other.

Informing the general public, interest groups, and stockholders of an organization's policies, activities, and accomplishments is an important part of a public relations specialist's job. The work also involves keeping management aware of public attitudes and the concerns of the many groups and organizations with which they must deal.

• **Salesperson.** Presenting the product to customers (individual or corporate), providing after-sale support with training or other services, disseminating product information, and recording sales information for later statistical analysis all fall under the umbrella of sales. Primary duties of salespeople are to interest wholesale and retail buyers and purchasing agents in their merchandise and to address any of the client's questions or concerns.

• **International marketer.** This is an area where working within the framework of different legal, social, and cultural traditions; obtaining translations where necessary; and consulting native or experienced personnel for guidance in both management of the company as well as marketing expertise are important. International marketing deals with market entry, segmentation, positioning, pricing, channel development, customer service, and globalization.

• **Retailer.** Retail involves working for commission on the sales floor, buying merchandise for a department or customer segment, coordinating and executing displays, analyzing sales figures for merchandising trends and direction, and managing the functions of a department, branch, or division. Retail salespeople assist customers in finding what they are looking for and try to interest them in buying the merchandise. They describe a product's features, demonstrate its use, or show various models and colors. For some sales jobs, particularly those involving expensive and complex items, retail salespeople need special knowledge or skills.

• **Consumer psychologist.** These psychologists are interested both in studying the psychological and social aspects of purchasing and consumption and in analyzing statistical data and making recommendations for application of the findings. The goals of consumer psychologists are to describe, predict, influence, and/or explain consumer responses.

• **Product manager.** Coordinating all aspects of an individual item or group of product offerings and overseeing production, advertising, public relations, distribution, sales, and pricing fall into this category.

• **Direct marketer.** This specialty involves using one or more advertising media to generate a measurable response from actual or potential customers and providing all of the information necessary for the prospective buyer to make a purchase decision and to complete the transaction.

• **Marketing educator.** Teaching groups of businesspeople the latest techniques and practices; contributing to and staying abreast of developments in the field; and working with practitioners to analyze and refine real-world applications are all a part of marketing education.

• **Marketing manager.** Understanding marketing planning and strategy, as well as how to use marketing technology to launch a new product or boost the marketing and sales efforts behind a company's existing products, are the responsibilities of those in marketing management.

• **Project manager.** These specialists are involved in getting input on what has to be done and then figuring out how to get it done. They accomplish this by rounding up the appropriate resources, managing the creative development, supervising production, and working closely with printers and mail houses to ensure that the completed work gets out the door on time.

• **Brand manager.** Knowing how the whole integrated marketing package comes together—including advertising, direct mail, online, publicity, special events, and other tactics—is the responsibility of the branding specialist. Also necessary is knowing what services are required from outside agencies and how to manage those agencies to achieve a consistent brand message over a wide assortment of channels.

Forms of Marketing

Within the above disciplines there are further divisions: consumer versus industrial; products versus services and ideas; and profit versus nonprofit/charitable. In the real world, these disciplines can and often do exist in combinations, such as nonprofit consumer services or for-profit industrial ideas.

Although these areas will be treated separately for the sake of clarity, bear in mind that in the real world such distinctions do not always exist. You will likely find, especially in smaller organizations, that marketing responsibility encompasses several of the above areas without separating the functions, such as advertising and public relations, for example.

One trend in marketing is toward reliance on quantification, that is, representing research findings or advertising responses as a numerical value. This tendency results in a scientific approach to marketing, emphasizing mathematical and statistical procedures. Another outcome of this trend is a broader information-based field that appeals to both the qualitative and quantitative mind.

2

MARKETING FIELDS

Now THAT YOU know a little more about marketing in general, it's time to find out what marketers actually do. We will describe typical jobs and their titles, from entry level to top executive. At the end of each field, you will find the names and addresses of the major professional organizations specific to that field, and where appropriate we have included the title of any publications available on careers in that field. Go to their websites or contact these organizations directly for more information. Most will gladly assist someone who is new to or interested in their specialty.

Research

Marketing research is that branch of marketing concerned with finding out why and how. Why was a purchase made? How often? Will it be purchased again? If not why not? Where was the purchase made and why? What were the important attributes of the product—was it price, quality, place, or some combination? To what extent was price important? Place? What other factors influenced that purchase? Was it advertising? If so, where were the ads?

How do we obtain the answers to these questions? How do we get customers to answer accurately and meaningfully? How do we make sure we're asking the right questions? How do we implement our findings? All of these concerns are the territory of the marketing researcher.

There are two basic types of research:

• **Quantitative marketing research.** This is research used to statistically determine the viewpoints of a population, enabling marketers to predict buyer behavior. This research usually employs large samples and takes but short amounts of a respondent's time. Telephone, mail, intercept, door-to-door, Internet or Web surveys, central location tests, mystery shopping, and in-home use studies are all used in quantitative research.

• **Qualitative marketing research.** This is research that yields an in-depth understanding about an issue. Qualitative research typically focuses on a small number of people. Since these people are interviewed in-depth, interviews tend to be longer and are often unstructured. An outline of discussion points, rather than a questionnaire, is often used. This type of research tends to be conducted in person, either in focus groups or one-on-one interviews; however, the Internet is a growing medium for qualitative marketing research.

Jobs and Job Titles

• **Field coordinator.** This position oversees the field personnel who actively collect data, whether administering questionnaires in a shopping center, conducting telephone surveys, or observing focus groups. He or she ensures that accurate interview and research techniques are being employed, often codes and tabulates data, monitors the project's progress, reports any abnormalities or unusual situations, and is responsible for demonstrating the benefits of these products to consumers.

• **Project manager.** This manager handles the implementation of the entire research project from methodology to questionnaire design; oversees activity of field coordinators; obtains computer services for statistical analysis; interprets findings and produces reports for presentation to the client; is in charge of setting up focus groups, handling the logistics, assisting participants, and follow up; and assists with proposals, questionnaires, and billing.

• **Account representative/account executive.** This position directs client contact; obtains customers by presenting appropriate research techniques for the situation; interprets client needs and represents client to project manager; acts as liaison between client and project team, keeping client informed of progress and preliminary findings; and provides support to both client and project team at meetings. He or she also performs research into specific market sectors to determine opportunities for sales within target organizations and profiles those organizations; works with marketing in generation and qualification of new leads in specific market sectors; identifies projects for further qualification/customer visits and works with other team members to advance those projects; and works with channel partners to close targeted opportunities.

• **Research specialist.** This person generally operates in the context of an advertising agency or in-house marketing/advertising department within a large corporation; is an expert in statistics, research design, and mathematical modeling; oversees all research activity; and works with project managers to ensure suitability of methodology and statistical approach as well as validity of findings.

References

California Employment Development Department
800 Capitol Mall, MIC 83
Sacramento, CA 95814
http://www.edd.ca.gov

Chronicle Guidance Publications, Inc.
66 Aurora Street
Moravia, NY 13118-3569
http://www.chronicleguidance.com

Marketing Research Association
1344 Silas Deane Highway, Suite 306
Rocky Hill, CT 06067-1342
www.mra-net.org

Advertising

Does the excitement of working on Madison Avenue have you interested in a career in advertising? Do you want to work behind the scenes on a nationally televised commercial? These are only two of the many facets of advertising, and we will present a brief portrait of this glamorous field. If you are seriously considering an advertising career and would like a more in-depth discussion, read the book in this series entitled *Opportunities in Advertising Careers*.

Jobs and Job Titles

• **Account representative, account executive.** This position directs contact with the client; acts as liaison between art department, production department, and client; maintains communications among these groups; represents client's needs to art and production departments; provides interpretive support to client at presentations; and is responsible for seeing that client needs are met accurately and on time, which calls for closely following the in-house progress of the campaign.

• **Media buyer, media coordinator.** This person manages the purchase and control of large blocks of media time/space, whether in print or broadcast; recommends and allocates this space among clients according to campaign requirements; and negotiates favorable billing terms for large, repeat, and/or guaranteed space purchases, which translates into more cost-effectiveness for clients and agency. Many buyers also plan advertising campaigns. Advertising media buyers work for advertising agencies as consultants, advising clients as to which media should be used to best advertise a product or service.

• **Media analyst.** The media analyst applies statistical models to audience, circulation, and cost figures to minimize media cost and maximize media effectiveness and provides support for client campaign implementation. He or she acts as an information and research expert for both agency staff and external clients. The role involves preparing detailed media evaluation reports and taking responsibility for finding the answers to specific research questions that would lead to more effective marketing campaigns. Media analysts run qualitative and quantitative research.

• **Art director.** This position requires an art background and experience as a graphic or commercial artist. The art director supervises a staff of artists, paste-up artists, and printing/production technicians; develops and recommends artistic strategy and rendition for the client campaign, often presenting several for client approval; and oversees progression of the campaign from rough sketches through final production. Advertising art directors work on the visual side of advertising. As part of a creative team, they work closely with writers to create original ideas using a brief from the client. Their role is to interpret what the client wants to say in an interesting way. They are also responsible for engaging other members of the team, such as illustrators, photographers, designers, or Mac operators in the project.

• **Production manager.** This person coordinates the mechanical aspects of the campaign for print and broadcast media and oversees the quality of renditions and final form whether on paper, film, or tape. Responsibilities include overseeing all print production operations in conjunction with the role of key liaison between the sales department, clients, printers, and other third-party solution-providers.

• **Specialty advertising manager.** This manager recommends and obtains imprinted merchandise appropriate to a client's campaign; develops the strategy and recommends items to be used; and obtains sources and monitors production to ensure timely arrival. He or she develops advertising for the sales staff and customers or distributors.

• **Research specialist.** This person usually works in a large agency or in-house marketing/advertising department; is expert in statistical applications, mathematical modeling, project design, and methodology; works with and often obtains outside services; and monitors projects to ensure accuracy and validity of findings, which are then reported and presented to the client.

• **Traffic manager.** This is an ideal starting point because this position interacts with just about every aspect of advertising. The traffic manager coordinates all the jobs in process and monitors their status to ensure that production remains on schedule and deadlines are met.

"But I don't live in New York. How will I ever get started?" Major cities are loaded with advertising agencies, and many towns have their share of small shops willing to lend a hand with an apprenticeship or internship. If you are already in college and are studying in a related area such as marketing or communications, your placement office can be a good source of information on such openings. You can also look around campus at opportunities with the student newspaper or even the publicity department of the school itself for a chance to gain valuable experience assisting with advertising or related functions.

References

American Advertising Federation
1101 Vermont Avenue NW, Suite 500
Washington, DC 20005-6306
www.aaf.org

American Association of Advertising Agencies, Inc.
405 Lexington Avenue, 18th Floor
New York, NY 10174-1801
www.aaaa.org

Business Marketing Association
Business/Professional Advertising Association (BPAA)
400 North Michigan Avenue, 15th Floor
Chicago, IL 60611
www.marketing.org

The Fashion Institute of Design and Merchandising (FIDM)
919 South Grand Avenue
Los Angeles, CA 90015-1421
http://www.fidm.com

Graphic Arts Technical Foundation
200 Deer Run Road
Sewickley, PA 15143
http://www.gatf.org

Field, Shelly. *Career Opportunities in Advertising and Public Relations*, (Career Opportunities Series). New York: Facts on File, Inc., 1997.

Flecker, Sally A. and Pamela J. Groff. *Careers in Graphic Communications: A Resource Book*. Sewickley, Pa.: GATF Press, 1998.

Hameroff, Eugene J. *Advertising Agency Business: The Complete Manual for Management and Operation*. Lincolnwood, Ill.: NTC/Contemporary Publishing Group, Inc., 1997.

Morgan, Bradley J. (editor). *Advertising Career Directory*. Farmington Hills, Mich.: Visible Ink Press, 1992.

Pattis, S. William. *Careers in Advertising*. Chicago: McGraw-Hill, 2004.

Public Relations

You've probably heard the term public relations, but do you know what it really means and how and why companies use it? Public relations (PR) is, literally, the relationship of the company with the public it serves including customers, employees, stockholders, and the community. As companies are in the public eye, they make every effort to ensure that the public is aware of the positive aspects of their businesses, which might otherwise go unnoticed. This is the task of the PR department—to see that the press is notified of new product introductions, favorable investment performance, employees promoted or hired, company-supported community projects, and similar newsworthy events.

Jobs and Job Titles

• **PR assistant.** This is an entry-level position at which one performs mostly behind-the-scenes activities such as writing routine press releases; coordinating luncheons and special events by reserving the room or site, ordering the meal, arranging for the speaker, ensuring attendance, and providing press coverage; and basically attending to the details involved in carrying out the corporate or client's public relations goals.

• **PR manager.** This position develops and implements the PR program at the corporate level (or for clients), coordinating the activities of PR assistants with those of other departments. Public relations managers also evaluate advertising and promotion programs for compatibility with public relations efforts and serve as the eyes and ears of top management. They observe social, economic, and political trends that might ultimately affect the firm and make recommendations to enhance the firm's image based on those trends. They assist company executives in drafting speeches, arranging interviews, and maintaining other forms of public contact; oversee company archives; and respond to information requests. In addition, some handle special events such as sponsorship of races, parties introducing new products, or other activities the firm supports to gain public attention through the press without advertising directly.

• **Community relations manager.** Usually in the largest organizations, this position is directly involved with activities in the community in which the corporation is located. By lending financial and/or personnel support to community-based causes, the organization helps those groups remain viable and contributes to the stability of the community. In addition, the organization gains credibility and favorable press coverage for its civic-mindedness. The community relations manager plans, coordinates, and facilitates strategic advertising in local media outlets to include newspapers, radio, and/or television, and serves as liaison to local, state, and federal government agencies on community relations issues.

• **Community relations director.** The community relations director evaluates various opportunities for community involvement and works with representatives from those organizations to develop appropriate programs for corporate sponsorship. The person in this position is responsible for the community's internal and external sales efforts.

References

Public Relations Society of America
33 Maiden Lane, 11th Floor
New York, NY 10038-5150
www.prsa.org

Morgan, Bradley J. *Public Relations Career Directory: A Practical One-Stop Guide to Getting a Job in Public Relations.* Farmington Hills, Mich.: Gale Research, Inc., 1993.
Rotman, Morris B. *Opportunities in Public Relations Careers.* Lincolnwood, Ill.: NTC/Contemporary Publishing Group, Inc., 2001.

Sales and Sales Management

This is the area most people associate with marketing. In a sales job you are representing your company and its products to your customer on a one-to-one basis. You must know your products and how they perform; you also must know your competitors' products and how they compare to yours.

Jobs and Job Titles

• **Market representative, account executive, salesperson, sales representative.** This is an entry-level position that often involves a training program in the larger organizations. In smaller organizations, an apprenticeship of sorts is more the rule. People in these positions accompany experienced salespeople at first and then move on to their own territories to visit clients, develop new business, and market their company's products.

• **Sales manager (area, group, product or product line, district, regional, national).** The sales manager directs the activities of the sales force, which involves coordinating with other departments in the firm, such as marketing and advertising, so that special promotions and new products are supported in the field. Monitoring sales performance and forecasting sales figures are also part of the job. Sales managers direct the firm's sales program. They assign sales territories, set goals, and establish training programs for the sales representatives.

Managers advise the sales representatives on ways to improve their sales performance. In large, multiproduct firms, they oversee regional and local sales managers and their staffs. Sales managers maintain contact with dealers and distributors. They analyze sales statistics gathered by their staffs to determine sales potential and inventory requirements and monitor the preferences of customers. Such information is vital in order to develop products and maximize profits.

• **Sales director (area, group, product or product line, district, regional, national).** This position oversees all of the sales activities of several groups or sales managers and is often responsible for their profitability. The sales director ensures the cooperation of other departments with the sales effort, as well as sales support of promotional activities. Vice president of sales or sales and marketing (area, group, product line, district, region, or national) is very often the next step up the ladder after serving as sales director. The VP is responsible for managing a team of sales executives, including hiring, training, and coaching. Additionally, he or she develops a sales plan to meet or exceed all objectives, ensuring that the sales funnel is sufficient to achieve these revenue objectives.

References

American Marketing Association
250 South Wacker Drive, Suite 5800
Chicago, IL 60606
www.marketingpower.com

National Retail Federation (NRF)
325 Seventh Street NW, Suite 1000
Washington, DC 20004
www.nrf.com

Sales and Marketing Executives International
P.O. Box 1390
Sumas, WA 98295-1390
www.smei.org

International Marketing

International marketing has come of age as our business environment is more worldwide than ever. With today's emphasis on multinational corporations and balance of trade between countries, the international marketer is very much in the thick of things in the global marketplace.

International marketers will generally begin their careers in another area of the marketing function and then transfer to the international department after gaining some experience. One way to speed up the process is to establish fluency in a foreign language, specifically that of a country in which your company is doing business.

Jobs and Job Titles

• **International specialist.** This is usually an experienced marketer who has knowledge of the country in which the company is interested. This person should be familiar not only with the language but the culture and legal climate as well. Often people in this position are native to the foreign country and have lived and worked in America to gain experience in this market. This does not preclude an American person working in international marketing, but it serves to point up the importance of immersion in the other country's culture. International specialists execute international promotional and marketing communication programs and research and interpret international market trends and opportunities unique to the industry.

• **Director of international marketing.** This director coordinates all overseas marketing activities and generally lives and works abroad. He or she frequently takes on diplomatic overtones as business relationships in and with other countries often are as carefully negotiated as political ties. The director provides a key contact point within the organization for problem solving operational issues; is the leader for the assessment and forecasting of key business development opportunities; leads and/or participates in the strategic and brand planning processes for the region; and manages key work streams as identified by the regional leadership team in carrying out regional initiatives.

Reference

Arpan, Jeffrey. *Opportunities in International Business Careers.*
   Lincolnwood, Ill.: NTC Publishing Group, Inc., 1995.

Retailing and Merchandising

Retailing and merchandising are more than just selling; planning
and forecasting are a big part of the job, too.

A career in retailing used to consist of a few positions, beginning in the stockroom and progressing to salesperson on the floor,
then moving up to store manager. The only promotion after that
required buying the store. Times have indeed changed, and today
one can work for a regional or national chain or one that special-
izes in a particular type of merchandise. You can specialize, too, in
operations or merchandising, and many store executives have experience in a broad spectrum of store functions.

Jobs and Job Titles

• **Buyer (junior, assistant, senior).** Beginning as a junior buyer,
one serves as an apprentice and learns the groundwork of the retailing business, such as calculating open-to-buy and dealing with different manufacturers, under the direction of the buyer (senior or
assistant, depending on the size of the company).

As an assistant buyer, one is given more responsibility while still
under the direction of another more experienced buyer. Often the
assistant will work with either a particular manufacturer or a merchandise line.

Once the position of buyer or senior buyer is attained, one is
usually responsible for purchases for a single department or mer-

chandise segment and oversees the activities of any junior or assistant buyers in that department. Buyers are responsible for understanding customers' needs and wants, monitoring competition, and working with vendors to select and purchase merchandise. They must constantly stay in contact with their stores by visiting them, by talking to sales associates and managers, and by monitoring the sales data available on their merchandise management systems. They also plan and implement sales promotion plans for their merchandise, such as arranging for advertising and ensuring that the merchandise is displayed properly.

• **Department manager.** This position coordinates buying activities for a given department; oversees day-to-day staffing, customer service, efficiency, orderliness, and merchandise display; and is responsible for longer-term buying projections and performance statistics, including the profitability of the department. A department manager is responsible for merchandise presentation, customer service, and inventory control for an area of the store. Store managers direct and coordinate the activities in these stores. They may set pricing policies to maintain profitability and notify senior management of concerns or problems. Store managers usually supervise department managers directly and oversee other store employees indirectly.

• **Merchandise manager.** This position oversees the purchasing of items in a broad group or category, such as housewares or men's apparel, and coordinates activities between departments under that category. The merchandise manager is also responsible for purchase and performance analysis, including the profitability of the merchandise group, and for the creation and execution of merchandising projects and marketing programs that are related to selected product lines. He or she also has to coordinate projects and assignments and communicate merchandising programs to internal departments.

• **Store/branch manager.** This position handles operations for all departments and merchandise lines at a given location, coordinates purchase and performance activities between buyers and managers, and is responsible for the profitability of the branch. Store management involves all the disciplines necessary to run a successful business, including sales planning and goal setting, overall store image and merchandise presentation, budgets and expense control, customer service and sales supervision, personnel administration and development, and community relations.

• **Regional (function) manager.** This manager oversees operations of several stores or branches for a given function such as purchasing or display. He or she is responsible for analyzing and accommodating local preferences and conditions, and for profitability of the region.

Regional managers recruit, train, and retain a qualified sales force and administrative personnel and ensure that standard operating procedures are being followed. They monitor branch sales managers, sales managers, and selling sales managers to ensure that these subordinates are following the responsibilities and procedures set forth; and they perform the quarterly forecasting and monthly business reviews.

• **General manager.** Based at headquarters, this position is responsible for all operations and profitability of the regions or branches.

• **Vice president (function or region).** Also based at headquarters, the VP oversees all function-related or regional activities. Again, profitability is a responsibility. This position is usually found in the larger retail organizations, where the vice president oversees the development and growth of client accounts and branch staff, works with the management team to set the direction for the office, and provides input and implements a corporate business plan at the local level to increase new business and further develop existing client relationships.

References

California Employment Development Department
800 Capitol Mall, MIC 83
Sacramento, CA 95814
http://www.edd.ca.gov

The Fashion Institute of Design and Merchandising (FIDM)
919 South Grand Avenue
Los Angeles, CA 90015-1421
http://www.fidm.com

National Retail Federation (NRF)
325 Seventh Street NW, Suite 1100
Washington, DC 20004
www.nrf.com

Occupational Outlook Service. *Occupational Outlook Handbook*, 2004–5 edition. Washington, DC: U.S. Department of Labor; http://stats.bls.gov/oco/ocos120.htm.

Consumer Psychology

Consumer psychology attempts to understand how customers make purchase decisions—what they buy and why. This area often works closely with marketing research to develop questionnaires that will elicit accurate responses and develop meaningful data. The consumer psychologist studies how consumers think, how they select from among alternative products, how they process product information, how they respond to their environment relative to purchasing, and why they buy products.

Jobs and Job Titles

• **Analyst.** Usually in an advertising agency or a large consumer package-goods company, this position provides understanding of what motivates consumers to purchase an item. This information helps the company decide how best to reach its intended customer, as well as gives insight to what people want in a product. Analysts develop data driven, multichannel marketing programs by generating in-depth analysis and interpretation of customer demographic, psychographic, and transactional data.

• **Specialist.** This field is prime for entrepreneurs, and those who are involved are often research oriented. A popular career choice in this area is education. Specialists review data; analyze and interpret results; write concise, insightful, actionable reports; and are proficient in demonstrating data in graphic format.

• **Educator.** Many consumer behaviorists can be found teaching marketing and consumer behavior at the college level while pursuing their research in the field. This can be an ideal position for the consumer psychologist.

Reference

www.consumerpsychologist.com

Product Management

This area of marketing requires a broad understanding of other business functions such as production, accounting, and distribution. You will work closely with people from these and other departments to manage your new product's development, test marketing, refining, formal introduction, and rollout. These same groups will also be necessary to keep your existing product on the market, updating it as necessary to meet changing demand and ultimately retiring it when the market for it declines. At the same time, the new product manager may introduce a replacement for the retired product.

Jobs and Job Titles

• **Assistant product manager.** This entry-level position works with the product manager, handling only certain product-related functions that are often in the form of special projects such as cooperative advertising or sales promotion. He or she is involved in planning for various product lines, promoting products through trade shows and product demonstrations, and helping with product training and distribution strategies.

• **Product manager.** This manager is responsible for all product-related functions and must see to it that activities are coordinated and that the product involved stays aligned with corporate goals. Profit accountability begins here. This manager assists in the identification and specification of new products and prepares marketing development requests. He or she also participates in competitive analysis and the development of competitive counterstrategies for new and existing products.

• **Group manager.** This position oversees a line of related products and their managers, with responsibility similar to that of the product manager but on a larger scale. He or she is responsible for improvement activities with the production team and provides training, mentoring, and improvement programs to the production teams.

• **Regional manager.** The regional manager is responsible for all product-related or line-related activities in a given geographical area and must ensure that the activities of the product and/or group managers adhere to strategic goals for the area. Duties also include growing the assigned territory, generating new business, and motivating and training staff and sales teams.

• **Division manager.** The division manager handles the complete line of related products or product groups on a national level. Accountable for productivity as well as profitability on a national level, this position coordinates the activities of several group and/or regional managers.

• **Division vice president.** Ultimate product responsibility rests here along with corporate goal setting and strategy implementation.

Reference

Association of International Product Marketing and Management
P.O. Box 1113
Palo Cedro, CA 96073
www.aipmm.com

Services Marketing

When a product is not a tangible product, how do you demonstrate that yours is better? More than ever, our economy is based on services like advertising, consulting, or word processing rather than on hard goods or products. As technology improves and manufacturing decreases, there is less demand for products and more demand for the after-sales support and follow-through that helps to differentiate one company from another. Although similar to product marketing in function and areas of responsibility, the challenge of services marketing lies in the intangible nature of a service and the ongoing usage of this kind of "product."

Jobs and Job Titles

• **Manager (assistant).** Much like its counterpart in product marketing, this position must coordinate all activities (promotion, production, and so forth) for the given service. In addition, the services marketing manager must ensure that follow-up and after-sale support is thorough and effective to maintain a positive relationship with the customers.

• **Group manager.** This position oversees several related services and coordinates all related activities, ensures that the efforts of the services managers are cohesive and are pulling in the same direction, is responsible for productivity and profitability of the total group, maintains a strong focus on client needs and establishes positive working relationships with clients, and maintains a focus on the environment, which may affect changing client needs.

• **Division manager.** The division manager handles the coordination of several groups of related services, ensuring that corporate goals are met and activities are unified. He or she will provide leadership and coordination of all human resource and program issues.

• **Regional manager.** This position is similar to that of the division manager, but for an assigned geographical area. The regional manager must ensure responsiveness to regional differences while complying with the corporate strategy. He or she also provides ongoing assessment of all staffing needs regionally and recommends changes as necessary.

• **Vice president.** This position encompasses responsibility for several divisions or regions and oversees primarily the financial and productivity areas, relying on the lower levels to provide follow-up and responsiveness to the customer. The VP is responsible for meeting the annual financial plan.

Reference

Information Technology Services Marketing Association
Lexington Office Park
420 Bedford Street, Suite 110
Lexington, MA 02420
www.itsma.com

Nonprofit Marketing

There are many national nonprofit associations, and these organizations tend to be smaller and more localized than their counterparts in industry. Of necessity, staff size is often minimal, and each position frequently holds more responsibility than might otherwise be expected. There is usually a high degree of interaction with the community—from individuals to industries. As a result, a job with a nonprofit organization or agency can be exceptionally challenging as well as fulfilling.

Jobs and Job Titles

• **Assistant or coordinator.** This entry-level position works with the marketing or development director and is responsible for the nuts and bolts of a particular campaign, whether for membership or fund-raising. Assistants are often involved in special projects requiring research and interpretive skills. Other responsibilities include editing and formatting correspondence, organizing meetings, and scheduling travel arrangements.

• **Marketing director.** This position develops the campaign and oversees its implementation, often coordinating the activities of a large staff of volunteers. Thus marketing directors frequently require specialized knowledge of nonprofit associations and community relations. They handle public relations issues if the organization does not have a PR department or consultant and are in charge of all marketing activities for the organization.

• **Development director.** Because the development director is responsible for fund-raising, he or she must be skilled in market development and have experience in financial goal setting. This person must cultivate close ties with the community, both corporate and individual, and work with a volunteer staff and coordinate its activities. The job involves organizing, managing, and directing the fund-raising campaigns; maintaining the financial resources of the nonprofit organization; and event planning.

• **Executive director.** This is the ultimate nonprofit position with responsibility for all functions of the organization from fund-raising to public relations to community involvement. It requires not only good business sense but also an outgoing, gregarious personality. The executive director is responsible for developing and maintaining relationships with other community agencies as well as the hiring, training, supervision, and evaluation of all staff members and programs.

• **Event coordinator.** One of the key methods of raising donations and funds for the nonprofit organization is through some form of special event. The event coordinator is responsible for all aspects of the event, ranging from initial planning to its implementation and promotion.

Reference

American Fund Raising Institute
http://www.afri.org

Direct Marketing

Direct marketing involves reaching customers without using a retailer. This type of marketing takes many forms, some of which you are probably already familiar with. No doubt you've received catalogs through the mail and possibly even answered telemarketing calls made by computers. These are but two of the many methods producers of products and services use to reach the customer directly. One of the newest methods ties in with cable television. Called electronic shopping, this medium allows the customer to make credit-card purchases via cable (usually telephone lines) through services that offer a wide variety of products and ship directly to the purchaser. Internet marketing currently accounts for some 25 percent of all retail purchases that are made in the United States.

Jobs and Job Titles

• **Specialist.** In this position you would be responsible for promoting the use of your company's shopping service to both the customer and the producer. Determining which promotional methods would be most effective and implementing a campaign to reach your market goal are important objectives of the specialist. Responsibilities include managing all aspects of program budgets; coordinating the rollout of multiple, concurrent direct marketing programs from idea generation to completion; and supporting the management of outside vendor relationships.

• **Manager.** This position is similar to that of the product manager in that it sets goals for market share and profitability. This manager handles the administrative functions of coordinating with other important areas like advertising, sales, and research and development; designs, develops, and implements direct marketing programs that stimulate profitable revenue growth in the organization; and manages and develops customer loyalty communications.

• **Director.** This is typically a semitechnical position requiring thorough knowledge of the latest innovations in electronics and software as well as awareness of customer response to these developments. The ability to apply these updates or recommend modifications to increase the appeal of current offerings would enhance performance in this position. People in this position develop and create direct response campaigns including direct mail, Web, and e-mail; analyze performance and strategies including mail response rates and return on investment; and develop and write copy for direct marketing campaigns.

References

Direct Marketing Association
1120 Avenue of the Americas
New York, NY 10036-6700
www.the-dma.org

Direct Selling Association
1275 Pennsylvania Avenue NW, Suite 800
Washington DC 20004
www.dsa.org

Business-to-Business (Industrial) Marketing

What's different when the customer is an organization? One difference is that you are often selling to a group, and you must understand the dynamics of that group. Or, in other cases, you must penetrate several layers of people before reaching the decision maker. While there are similarities to consumer marketing, businesspeople need to be treated differently, as is appropriate when single purchases represent large amounts of money and major budget items. Business-to-business marketing also tends to be more technical in nature and requires technical product knowledge often exceeding that of consumer marketers. In many cases your customer will know as much about your product as you do. As your product can affect how people perform their jobs, each purchase is carefully considered.

Jobs and Job Titles

• **Account representative/sales representative.** As in consumer marketing, this position involves calling on existing and potential customers for the purpose of persuading them to purchase your company's product. However, in industrial marketing, you will most likely be talking to a group of people who are all involved in the purchase decision, and each will have individual criteria for the product or service you represent. In many cases you will need a technical background to fully understand your customers' needs. Generating new business requires prospecting and identifying qualified leads through cold calling and referrals. Servicing accounts requires making persuasive presentations to business owners and decision makers.

• **Marketing manager.** This manager is responsible for the overall marketing effort for a company's product offerings and for the productivity and profitability of its marketing activities. Marketing managers must be familiar with the industry in general and the needs of their customers in particular; they must also identify and develop strong industry relationships and consistently strive to stay abreast of new trends and identify potential new product/service offerings to keep the company ahead of the competition. He or she will also manage the development of a sales marketing plan, complete with revenue goals and customer profiles; work closely with the new business team to research and target potential customers; develop monthly prospecting goals and organize sales presentations; and manage all aspects of the company's trade show activities.

• **Sales manager.** This position oversees the activities of the sales force and coordinates those activities with the other related departments, such as advertising and marketing. Sales managers have profit and productivity responsibility for the sales effort. They often accompany salespeople on calls to major clients, establish business relationships with these customers, negotiate media buys, and determine the strategic direction for various products.

• **Divisional sales/marketing manager.** This position coordinates the sales/marketing activities within a given product-line group or geographic region. Responsibilities include profitability and productivity, setting market and/or sales goals, monitoring progress of the company and its competitors in the field, hiring and managing representatives, developing relationships with key accounts, and achieving sales results by motivating representatives to meet territory goals.

References

Business Marketing Association
400 North Michigan Avenue, 15th Floor
Chicago, IL 60611
www.marketing.org

Elance Online
www.elanceonline.com

Marketing Education

Teaching at the college level is available in all areas (professional and geographic) and offers an exciting opportunity to share and apply learned marketing skills. Teaching requires advanced degrees, an M.B.A. or equivalent in a related field, plus enrollment in a Ph.D. program.

Jobs and Job Titles

• **Adjunct lecturer.** This typically part-time position (often evenings) generally requires only an M.B.A. or some master's degree at most schools.

• **Instructor.** The entry-level designation for full-time faculty, this position requires enrollment in a Ph.D. program as demonstration of serious commitment to the field.

• **Assistant professor.** Promotion to this level is usually contingent upon completion of Ph.D. course work, but it is often granted when the doctorate is earned. Assistant professors teach undergraduate/graduate courses, conduct research and other scholarly activities, establish partnerships with industries, and mentor students.

• **Associate professor.** The associate professor must have a Ph.D. (or equivalent) and continued employment is contingent upon contribution to the school and the field. He or she also assists with program and curriculum development.

• **Full professor.** Promotion to this position requires continued service, high-level research, involvement in the profession, and contributions to the field.

• **Department chair.** This administrative position is often rotated among department members. The department chair implements procedures to maintain and/or improve student retention, participates in curriculum and course development and revision, supervises and manages faculty performance, and works with admissions, student services, registrar, financial aid, and other departments to facilitate a team approach to building efficient and effective academic programs.

• **Dean.** The dean is typically the administrator of the school or department of business, and this is often in conjunction with teaching responsibilities. Further advancement takes place either in administration or in professional activities, such as publishing. The dean assists in overall campus planning; recruits, hires, trains, and develops instructional staff; observes and evaluates faculty; reviews curricula; and submits appropriate materials to the accrediting commission.

Reference

Marketing Education Association
P.O. Box 27473
Tempe, AZ 85285-7473
www.nationalmea.org

Consulting

Consulting is available in almost any area of marketing and is limited only by your skills and experience. This is not an entry-level position, but after developing your expertise, consulting offers an excellent opportunity to see many companies in action and learn how a variety of industries operate.

Jobs and Job Titles

• **Consultant.** Whether independent or in partnership, flexibility and independence are major advantages, along with the opportunity to be your own boss. Consulting can be and often is a second job until enough of a practice is built up to support full-time activity. Consultants serve as consumer-focused experts. In essence, they provide the voice of the customer.

3

EDUCATION AND TRAINING

How MUCH EDUCATION is enough? What should you study? What other disciplines are important? There are also differences in opinion between those who emphasize education and others who prefer experience in the field. Still others believe that only a business education is appropriate for a career in marketing, while some believe a liberal arts background is more rounded. Who has the answers to these questions? Nobody and everybody, which is another way of saying only you can decide what's better for you and your career. Let's look at some of the possibilities.

The Bachelor's Degree

The aim of an undergraduate education is to develop an individual who can think independently, who can communicate effectively, and who has been exposed to a common body of knowledge that forms the basis of our culture as well as that of others. At this level the emphasis is on the broad concepts, the understanding of how and why a particular theory functions, and the foundations of various disciplines rather than the depth of the specialist. Another outcome is a systematic approach to problem solving—a rational, logical process rather than unfocused, random methods—and the ability to apply basic mathematical and communication skills.

Even though you may be absolutely fascinated by marketing and want to spend your college career immersed in the field, restrain yourself and get a well-rounded education. This is your chance to become an educated individual. The importance of the liberal arts cannot be understated; they will help you develop your communications abilities, work on the analytical skills, and learn as much as you can about our world. In fact, most good undergraduate business programs require a balanced course of study, and actual course work in marketing generally does not begin until the junior year, after you have already been exposed to other disciplines. Remember, nothing exists in a vacuum. Even though a particular course, such as art history, may not seem relevant to you as a business major, it is still a part of the cultural context in which you will operate as a marketer, and it will inevitably take its place in your professional development.

Businesspeople cite communication and interpersonal skills as the areas college graduates most need to improve. Writing is an extremely important skill, and the time to learn is while you are in school where there are experts to teach you. If you have trouble with grammar, spelling, or sentence structure, now is the time to get help. Enroll in a remedial class if your school offers one. Remember, a poorly written document detracts from your professional image as much as does wearing scruffy clothes to the office.

School is also the place to learn by making mistakes, so take advantage of campus organizations to develop your leadership style and refine your people skills. Learn how to work with other individuals and groups; develop some diplomacy and practice using tact—you will find it much more effective and much less offensive than unbridled bluntness. Remember, it's not what you say but how you say it. You can accomplish more with other people when they are not put off by your manner.

The college and local chapters of the American Marketing Association are good places to begin and may be augmented by membership in specialized societies in management, public relations, advertising, and the like. Belonging to such groups as an undergraduate also reflects favorably on your commitment to the field and is not overlooked by potential employers.

Sample Undergraduate Program

The following recommended course of study for a bachelor's degree in marketing can be found at most major business schools The total number of required credits are 122.

Freshman Year—Required Credits: 31
English Composition (6)
Pre-Calculus Math (3)
Calculus (3)
Introduction to Computer Applications (1)
Principles of Macroeconomics (3)
Liberal Arts Electives (15)

Sophomore Year—Required Credits: 31
Financial Accounting (3)
Managerial Accounting (3)
Principles of Microeconomics (3)
Intermediate Microeconomic Analysis (3)
Legal Environment of Business (3)
Introduction to Management Information Systems (3)

Business Statistics (3)
Quantitative Analysis for Business Decisions (3)
Liberal Arts Electives (7)

Junior Year—Required Credits: 30
Managing Organizational Behavior (3)
Operations Management (3)
Marketing Management (3)
Business Finance (3)
Consumer Behavior (3)
Any One Marketing Elective (3)
Approved Electives (12)

Senior Year—Required Credits: 30
Managerial Strategy and Policy (3)
Marketing Research (3)
Marketing Strategy (3)
Any Three Marketing Electives (9)
Approved Electives (12)

Marketing electives—each of which is worth three credit hours—
include:

Advertising Strategies and Management
Business Marketing
Consumer Behavior
Direct Marketing
Health Care Marketing
Independent Marketing Study
International Field Study in Marketing
Internship in Marketing
Introduction to Advertising

Marketing Communications
Marketing on the Internet
Marketing in Not-for-Profit Organizations
Marketing Research
Marketing Strategy
Merchandising
Multinational Marketing
Personal Selling and Sales Management
Public Relations
Retail Management
Special Topics in Marketing

The M.B.A.

With good reason, one of the most often asked questions is, "Do I really need an M.B.A.?" It follows that the next question is, "Do most companies require one?"

In most situations, the answer to such questions depends on your undergraduate education, your employer's requirements, and especially on your personal and professional goals. What kind of work do you want to do and for what size company? Do you have a bachelor's degree in business? If so, did you concentrate in marketing? If you are employed in the field, you can determine better how much an M.B.A. would enhance your knowledge and ability to perform your current job or perhaps even prepare you for advancement.

The M.B.A. is a longer, harder look at the quantitative skills: the statistical techniques are more sophisticated and the analytical approaches are more complex. This is the level at which you concentrate on the field. Whether you generalize or specialize in marketing may depend on the nature of your undergraduate degree. Someone who concentrated in marketing at the undergraduate level may wish to round out that education by taking a generalist business degree or an M.B.A. in finance or management information systems (M.I.S.).

This is a good time to point out that most good M.B.A. programs require business experience, preferably at least two years' worth, prior to entering the program. This gives you the opportunity to gain some exposure to concrete examples of concepts you will encounter during your graduate studies, as well as allow you to test the waters to make certain the M.B.A. is right for you.

Although the M.B.A. has become increasingly popular due to its perceived glamour and the higher salaries some graduates command, a word of caution is in order. Because the sheer number of M.B.A.s awarded has grown so rapidly, the value of the degree to any person or organization is more and more related to individual circumstances than to the degree itself. Above the entry level, an M.B.A. is certainly desirable and may be required for advancement to upper management in certain organizations. At the very least it should help you refine the decision-making skills you have developed at the undergraduate level and on the job—if not provide you with a whole set of new skills.

In addition, if the organization requires you to have an M.B.A., or at least desires it, there may be some financial assistance, such as tuition abatement, to you as an employee. This is another reason to consider working for several years before pursuing the degree.

Does an M.B.A. lead to a higher salary? Generally, but not always. What is more likely to occur is that enhanced job performance is rewarded and promotions earned more quickly than without the M.B.A. Also, more doors may be opened and more opportunities available with the degree than without. Again, your individual goals come into play by suggesting which direction you should take, and only you can decide whether to pursue this form of graduate education. However, for serious marketing practitioners, the M.B.A. is a valuable tool and should be viewed as such.

Within the schools granting the M.B.A. there is considerable variation in teaching methods—each with advantages and drawbacks—the effectiveness of which will vary with the student. These techniques run the gamut from full-lecture to full-case method, with every possible combination along the way. A thorough investigation of the teaching philosophy of any M.B.A. programs you might consider is necessary to ensure optimal gain from the educational experience. Some schools offer learn-by-doing (also called co-op) opportunities with local businesses or internships in conjunction with established training programs, both of which provide unique hands-on experience in applying the skills and concepts learned in the academic side of the program. Ask about such possibilities when considering an M.B.A. program. Again, the appropriateness will depend on individual circumstances, personal objectives, and work experience.

The following is a list of the typical courses you may expect to encounter in an M.B.A. program. The average number of credits appears in parentheses.

Business Core Requirements (40 hours) Include
Financial Accounting
Managerial Accounting
Emerging Global Issues in Business
Social and Ethical Responsibility
Exploring the Dynamics of Leadership
Information Systems in Organizations
Small Business Enterprise
Principles of Economics
Applied Calculus

Legal Environment of Business
Business Finance
Introduction to Marketing Management
Statistical Reasoning
Business Organization and Management
Operations Management
Organizational Strategy

Advanced Required Courses (9 hours) Include
Buyer Behavior
Marketing Research
Strategic Marketing Management
Leadership and Management
Managing Technology
Managing Customer Interfaces
Business Law and Society: The Global Environment

Marketing Elective Courses (9 hours) Include
Foundations of Integrated Marketing Communication
Personal Selling and Relationship Marketing
Summer Study Abroad
Independent Study
Purchasing Policies and Procedures
Integrated Marketing Communication
Sales Management
Retailing Management and Promotion
Business-to-Business Marketing
Seminar in Marketing (topic varies)
International Marketing
Internship in Marketing
Advertising Management

Industrial Marketing
Market Planning and Corporate Strategy
Product Innovation and Development
Public Relations Management
Consumer Behavior

Some schools offer what is known as the "executive" or "intensive" M.B.A. program. Sometimes given on company premises, this type of program is geared toward the student who is already heavily involved in the business world and may have achieved mid- to upper-management status without the benefit of specialized education. Such a program usually schedules classes on weekends or during brief but intense periods dedicated only to academic activity. Some require sponsorship by one's firm and may be tailored to the needs of that particular organization; others are open to all.

As far as companies requiring an M.B.A. are concerned, a general rule is: the larger the organization, the more likely it is to prefer that its management level employees possess an advanced degree. There are always exceptions, of course, and many large organizations make it easier for their employees to obtain the degree by offering such benefits as tuition reimbursement and flextime to accommodate class hours. Suffice it to say that you may find it easier to obtain a challenging career position if you have the M.B.A. behind you.

Another thorny issue is the prominence of the school granting your M.B.A. Again, only you can weigh the potential benefits against your academic and financial abilities as well as your personal and professional goals. Do you want to be the next whiz kid–vice president at a top New York advertising agency? Or is it your ambition to be the head of marketing research at a major consumer goods manufacturer?

The Doctorate

Did you ever wonder why someone would pursue an education at this level? Or has the idea intrigued you but you didn't know how you might use the degree? You can teach your subject at the college level and be stimulated by other intelligent minds; you can consult with organizations, employing your expertise in the field; you can conduct research in your area and contribute to the body of knowledge; or you can do just about any combination thereof. One of the attractions of obtaining the Ph.D. is the flexibility it affords in a career choice, as well as the intellectual challenge and the stimulation of being on the cutting edge of new developments in your field.

The Ph.D. program is usually specifically tailored to the individual's interests, as well as those of the faculty in the department. If you are interested in a Ph.D. degree, there is a list in Appendix A of those schools offering such a program. Contact the department head directly for the information you need.

AACSB International—The Association to Advance Collegiate Schools of Business

The Association to Advance Collegiate Schools of Business (AACSB) is a nonprofit association of educational institutions, businesses, and other groups whose mission is to "advance management education worldwide through accreditation and through leadership." This organization promotes the use of standardized and accurate descriptions of courses and programs in business, and member schools are required to meet strict criteria in faculty standards, program quality, available resources, continuous improvement, and achievement against the mission. Many nonmember schools also pattern their course offerings after the AACSB model to offer a course of study that includes exposure to all facets of the business world while allowing for a professional concentration such as marketing.

AACSB International provides programs for the education of faculty and administrators; conducts research about the field of management education; bridges connections between education and the corporate community on a variety of business school–related projects and initiatives; and publishes special reports on trends and issues within management education. In addition, AACSB International maintains close relationships with other business education associations all around the world. AACSB is recognized by the Council of Higher Education Accreditation (CHEA). As the primary national accrediting agency of bachelor's, master's, and doctoral degree programs in the business field, it maintains contact with the U.S. Department of Education in order to promote the value of accreditation and enhancement of management education on a global basis. Accreditation is a quality measure of business schools based on each school's own articulated mission and goals. The following standards for accreditation appear on AACSB's website under the heading "Accreditation." (It is reprinted here by permission.) Go to www.aacsb.edu to read the entire standards document.

Standards for Accreditation

1. The school publishes a mission statement or its equivalent that provides direction for making decisions. The mission statement derives from a process that includes the viewpoints of various stakeholders. The school periodically reviews and revises the mission statement as appropriate. The review process involves appropriate stakeholders. [MISSION STATEMENT]

2. The school's mission statement is appropriate to higher education for management and consonant with the mission of any institution of which the school is a part. The mission includes the production of intellectual contributions that advance the knowledge and practice of business and management. [MISSION APPROPRIATENESS]

3. The mission statement or supporting documents specify the student populations the school intends to serve. [STUDENT MISSION]

4. The school specifies action items that represent high priority continuous improvement efforts. [CONTINUOUS IMPROVEMENT OBJECTIVES]

5. The school has financial strategies to provide resources appropriate to, and sufficient for, achieving its mission and action items. [FINANCIAL STRATEGIES]

Participants' Standards

6. The policies for admission to business degree programs offered by the school are clear and consistent with the school's mission. [STUDENT ADMISSION]

7. The school has academic standards and retention practices that produce high-quality graduates. The academic standards and retention practices are consistent with the school's mission. [STUDENT RETENTION]

8. The school maintains a staff sufficient to provide stability and ongoing quality improvement for student support activities. Student support activities reflect the school's mission and programs and the students' characteristics. [STAFF SUFFICIENCY-STUDENT SUPPORT]

9. The school maintains a faculty sufficient to provide stability and ongoing quality improvement for the instructional programs offered. The deployment of faculty resources reflects the mission and programs. Students in all programs, majors, areas of emphasis, and locations have the opportunity to receive instruction from appropriately qualified faculty. [FACULTY SUFFICIENCY]

10. The faculty has, and maintains, intellectual qualifications and current expertise to accomplish the mission and to assure that this occurs, the school has a clearly defined process to evaluate individual faculty member's contributions to the school's mission. [FACULTY QUALIFICATIONS]

11. The school has well-documented and communicated processes in place to manage and support faculty members over the progression of their careers consistent with the school's mission. These include:

- Determining appropriate teaching assignments, intellectual expectations, and service workloads.
- Providing staff and other mechanisms to support faculty in meeting the expectations the school holds for them on all mission-related activities.
- Providing orientation, guidance, and mentoring.
- Undertaking formal periodic review, promotion, and reward processes.
- Maintaining overall plans for faculty resources.

[FACULTY MANAGEMENT AND SUPPORT]

12. The business school's faculty in aggregate, its faculty subunits, and individual faculty, administrators, and staff share responsibility to:

- Ensure adequate time is devoted to learning activities for all faculty members and students.
- Ensure adequate student-faculty contact across the learning experiences.
- Set high expectations for academic achievement and provide leadership toward those expectations.
- Evaluate instructional effectiveness and overall student achievement.
- Continuously improve instructional programs.
- Innovate in instructional processes.

[AGGREGATE FACULTY AND STAFF EDUCATIONAL RESPONSIBILITY]
13. Individual teaching faculty members:

- Operate with integrity in their dealings with students and colleagues.
- Keep their own knowledge current with the continuing development of their teaching disciplines.
- Actively involve students in the learning process.
- Encourage collaboration and cooperation among participants.
- Ensure frequent, prompt feedback on student performance.

[INDIVIDUAL FACULTY EDUCATIONAL RESPONSIBILITY]
14. Individual students:

- Operate with integrity in their dealings with faculty and other students.
- Engage the learning materials with appropriate attention and dedication.

- Maintain their engagement when challenged by difficult learning activities.
- Contribute to the learning of others.
- Perform to standards set by the faculty.

[STUDENT EDUCATIONAL RESPONSIBILITY]

Eligibility Procedures for AACSB International Accreditation
1. An institution seeking accreditation by AACSB must offer degree-granting programs in business or management.
2. Degree programs in business must be supported by continuing resources.
3. All degree programs in business offered by the institution in all locations will be reviewed simultaneously.
4. Consistent with its mission and its cultural context, the institution must demonstrate diversity in its business programs.
5. The institution or the business programs of the institution must establish expectations for ethical behavior by administrators, faculty, and students.
6. At the time of the initial accreditation, a majority of business graduates shall be from programs that have produced graduates during at least two years.

Assurance of Learning Standards

15. Management of curricula. The school uses well documented, systematic processes to develop, monitor, evaluate, and revise the substance and delivery of the curricula of degree programs and to assess the impact of the curricula on learning. Curriculum management includes inputs from all appropriate constituencies which may include faculty, staff, administrators, students, faculty from

non-business disciplines, alumni, and the business community served by the school.

The standard requires use of a systematic process for curriculum management but does not require any specific courses in the curriculum. Normally, the curriculum management process will result in an undergraduate degree program that includes learning experiences in such general knowledge and skill areas as:

- Communication abilities.
- Ethical understanding and reasoning abilities.
- Analytic skills.
- Use of information technology.
- Multicultural and diversity understanding.
- Reflective thinking skills.

Normally, the curriculum management process will result in undergraduate and master's level general management degree programs that will include learning experiences in such management-specific knowledge and skills areas as:

- Ethical and legal responsibilities in organizations and society.
- Financial theories, analysis, reporting, and markets.
- Creation of value through the integrated production and distribution of goods, services, and information.
- Group and individual dynamics in organizations.
- Statistical data analysis and management science as they support decision-making processes throughout an organization.

- Information technologies as they influence the structure and processes of organizations and economies, and as they influence the roles and techniques of management.
- Domestic and global economic environments of organizations.
- Other management-specific knowledge and abilities as identified by the school.

[MANAGEMENT OF CURRICULA]

16. Bachelor's or undergraduate level degree: Knowledge and skills. Adapting expectations to the school's mission and cultural circumstances, the school specifies learning goals and demonstrates achievement of learning goals for key general, management-specific, and/or appropriate discipline-specific knowledge and skills that its students achieve in each undergraduate degree program. [UNDERGRADUATE LEARNING GOALS]

17. The bachelor's or undergraduate level degree programs must provide sufficient time, content coverage, student effort, and student-faculty interaction to assure that the learning goals are accomplished. [UNDERGRADUATE EDUCATIONAL LEVEL]

18. Master's level degree in general management (e.g., M.B.A.) programs: Knowledge and skills. Participation in a master's level degree program presupposes the base of general knowledge and skills appropriate to an undergraduate degree. Learning at the master's level is developed in a more integrative, interdisciplinary fashion than undergraduate education. The capacities developed through the knowledge and skills of a general master's level program are:

- Capacity to lead in organizational situations.
- Capacity to apply knowledge in new and unfamiliar circumstances through a conceptual understanding of relevant disciplines.
- Capacity to adapt and innovate to solve problems, to cope with unforeseen events, and to manage in unpredictable environments.

Adapting expectations to the school's mission and cultural circumstances, the school specifies learning goals and demonstrates master's level achievement of learning goals for key management-specific knowledge and skills in each master's level general management program. [MASTER'S LEVEL GENERAL MANAGEMENT LEARNING GOALS]

19. Master's level degree in specialized programs: Knowledge and skills. Participation in a master's level program presupposes the base of general knowledge and skills appropriate to an undergraduate degree and is at a more advanced level.

The level of knowledge represented by the students of a specialized master's level program is the:

- Application of knowledge even in new and unfamiliar circumstances through a conceptual understanding of the specialization.
- Ability to adapt and innovate to solve problems.
- Capacity to critically analyze and question knowledge claims in the specialized discipline.

Master's level students in specialized degree programs demonstrate knowledge of theories, models, and tools relevant to their specialty field. They are able to apply appropriate specialized theories, models, and tools to solve concrete business and managerial problems. Adapting expectations to the school's mission and cultural circumstances, the school specifies learning goals and demonstrates achievement of learning goals in each specialized master's degree program. [SPECIALIZED MASTER'S DEGREE LEARNING GOALS]

20. The master's level degree programs must provide sufficient time, content coverage, student effort, and student-faculty interaction to assure that the learning goals are accomplished. [MASTER'S EDUCATIONAL LEVEL]

21. Doctoral level degree: Knowledge and skills. Doctoral programs educate students for highly specialized careers in academe or practice. Students of doctoral level programs demonstrate the ability to create knowledge through original research in their areas of specialization. Normally, doctoral programs will include:

- The acquisition of advanced knowledge in areas of specialization.
- The development of advanced theoretical or practical research skills for the areas of specialization.
- Explicit attention to the role of the specialization areas in managerial and organizational contexts.
- Preparation for teaching responsibilities in higher education (for those students who expect to enter teaching careers).
- Dissertation, or equivalent, demonstrating personal integration of, and original intellectual contribution to, a field of knowledge.
- Other areas as identified by the school.

[DOCTORAL LEARNING GOALS]

4

A CAREER IN MARKETING: HONEST WORK

BEFORE WE GO any further, let's discuss an extremely important issue—that of ethics, a code of conduct. Remember in the beginning of the book where we attempted to address some of the negative stereotypes of marketers? Well, the American Marketing Association (AMA), an organization dedicated to professionalism in marketing, has adopted a code of ethics to guide all those in the field in its practice and conduct. The code as it appears here was approved and adopted by the AMA in August 2004. As you read this document, consider how it opposes those negative stereotypes we talked about and in their place promotes a positive, honest approach to business in general. This code of ethics is quoted in its entirety and is reprinted with the permission of the American Marketing Association.

American Marketing Association Code of Ethics

Ethical Norms and Values for Marketers

Preamble

The American Marketing Association commits itself to promoting the highest standard of professional ethical norms and values for its members. Norms are established standards of conduct that are expected and maintained by society and/or professional organizations. Values represent the collective conception of what people find desirable, important and morally proper. Values serve as the criteria for evaluating the actions of others.

Marketing practitioners must recognize that they not only serve their enterprises but also act as stewards of society in creating, facilitating and executing the efficient and effective transactions that are part of the greater economy. In this role, marketers should embrace the highest ethical norms of practicing professionals and the ethical values implied by their responsibility toward stakeholders (e.g., customers, employees, investors, channel members, regulators and the host community).

General Norms

1. Marketers must do no harm. This means doing work for which they are appropriately trained or experienced so that they can actively add value to their organizations and customers. It also means adhering to all applicable laws and regulations and embodying high ethical standards in the choices they make.

2. Marketers must foster trust in the marketing system. This means that products are appropriate for their intended and pro-

moted uses. It requires that marketing communications about goods and services are not intentionally deceptive or misleading. It suggests building relationships that provide for the equitable adjustment and/or redress of customer grievances. It implies striving for good faith and fair dealing so as to contribute toward the efficacy of the exchange process.

3. Marketers must embrace, communicate and practice the fundamental ethical values that will improve consumer confidence in the integrity of the marketing exchange system. These basic values are intentionally aspirational and include honesty, responsibility, fairness, respect, openness and citizenship.

Ethical Values

1. **Honesty.** To be truthful and forthright in our dealings with customers and stakeholders.

- We will tell the truth in all situations and at all times.
- We will offer products of value that do what we claim in our communications.
- We will stand behind our products if they fail to deliver their claimed benefits.
- We will honor our explicit and implicit commitments and promises.

2. **Responsibility.** To accept the consequences of our marketing decisions and strategies.

- We will make strenuous efforts to serve the needs of our customers.

- We will avoid using coercion with all stakeholders.
- We will acknowledge the social obligations to stakeholders that come with increased marketing and economic power.
- We will recognize our special commitments to economically vulnerable segments of the market such as children, the elderly and others who may be substantially disadvantaged.

3. **Fairness.** To try to balance justly the needs of the buyer with the interests of the seller.

- We will represent our products in a clear way in selling, advertising and other forms of communication; this includes the avoidance of false, misleading and deceptive promotion.
- We will reject manipulations and sales tactics that harm customer trust.
- We will not engage in price fixing, predatory pricing, price gouging or "bait-and-switch" tactics.
- We will not knowingly participate in material conflicts of interest.

4. **Respect.** To acknowledge the basic human dignity of all stakeholders.

- We will value individual differences even as we avoid stereotyping customers or depicting demographic groups (e.g., gender, race, sexual orientation) in a negative or dehumanizing way in our promotions.
- We will listen to the needs of our customers and make all reasonable efforts to monitor and improve their satisfaction on an ongoing basis.

- We will make a special effort to understand suppliers, intermediaries and distributors from other cultures.
- We will appropriately acknowledge the contributions of others, such as consultants, employees and coworkers, to our marketing endeavors.

5. **Openness.** To create transparency in our marketing operations.

- We will strive to communicate clearly with all our constituencies.
- We will accept constructive criticism from our customers and other stakeholders.
- We will explain significant product or service risks, component substitutions or other foreseeable eventualities that could affect customers or their perception of the purchase decision.
- We will fully disclose list prices and terms of financing as well as available price deals and adjustments.

6. **Citizenship.** To fulfill the economic, legal, philanthropic and societal responsibilities that serve stakeholders in a strategic manner.

- We will strive to protect the natural environment in the execution of marketing campaigns.
- We will give back to the community through volunteerism and charitable donations.
- We will work to contribute to the overall betterment of marketing and its reputation.

- We will encourage supply chain members to ensure that trade is fair for all participants, including producers in developing countries.

Implementation

Finally, we recognize that every industry sector and marketing subdiscipline (e.g., marketing research, e-commerce, direct selling, direct marketing, advertising) has its own specific ethical issues that require policies and commentary. An array of such codes can be accessed through links on the AMA Web site. We encourage all such groups to develop and/or refine their industry and discipline-specific codes of ethics to supplement these general norms and values.

This code is a far cry from the "buyer beware" approach businesspeople are often accused of practicing. Think about how you might employ this code as both a marketer and a customer. See how other businesspeople are operating within the guidelines set down in the code and how an organization's reputation for honesty and accuracy can also help to improve its profitability. After all, what kind of product/service would you prefer? What kind of organization do you go back to time after time? What kind of individuals do you want to do business with? Won't your customers want the same of you and your organization?

And, as the field of marketing changes, largely due to the emerging technologies, new ethical questions arise. In response, the AMA has also developed a code of ethics for marketing on the Internet. It builds on the components and spirit of the original AMA Code of Ethics.

American Marketing Association Code of Ethics for Marketing on the Internet

http://www.ama.org/about/ama/ethcode.htm

Ethical Norms and Values for Marketers

Preamble

The American Marketing Association commits itself to promoting the highest standard of professional ethical norms and values for its members. Norms are established standards of conduct that are expected and maintained by society and/or professional organizations. Values represent the collective conception of what people find desirable, important and morally proper. Values serve as the criteria for evaluating the actions of others. Marketing practitioners must recognize that they not only serve their enterprises but also act as stewards of society in creating, facilitating and executing the efficient and effective transactions that are part of the greater economy. In this role, marketers should embrace the highest ethical norms of practicing professionals and the ethical values implied by their responsibility toward stakeholders (e.g., customers, employees, investors, channel members, regulators and the host community).

General Norms

1. Marketers must do no harm. This means doing work for which they are appropriately trained or experienced so that they can actively add value to their organizations and customers. It also means adhering to all applicable laws and regulations and embodying high ethical standards in the choices they make.

2. Marketers must foster trust in the marketing system. This means that products are appropriate for their intended and promoted uses. It requires that marketing communications about goods and services are not intentionally deceptive or misleading. It suggests building relationships that provide for the equitable adjustment and/or redress of customer grievances. It implies striving for good faith and fair dealing so as to contribute toward the efficacy of the exchange process.

3. Marketers must embrace, communicate and practice the fundamental ethical values that will improve consumer confidence in the integrity of the marketing exchange system. These basic values are intentionally aspirational and include honesty, responsibility, fairness, respect, openness and citizenship.

Ethical Values

1. **Honesty.** To be truthful and forthright in our dealings with customers and stakeholders.

- We will tell the truth in all situations and at all times.
- We will offer products of value that do what we claim in our communications.
- We will stand behind our products if they fail to deliver their claimed benefits.
- We will honor our explicit and implicit commitments and promises.

2. **Responsibility.** To accept the consequences of our marketing decisions and strategies.

- We will make strenuous efforts to serve the needs of our customers.

- We will avoid using coercion with all stakeholders.
- We will acknowledge the social obligations to stake-holders that come with increased marketing and economic power.
- We will recognize our special commitments to economically vulnerable segments of the market such as children, the elderly and others who may be substantially disadvantaged.

3. **Fairness.** To try to balance justly the needs of the buyer with the interests of the seller.

- We will represent our products in a clear way in selling, advertising and other forms of communication; this includes the avoidance of false, misleading and deceptive promotion.
- We will reject manipulations and sales tactics that harm customer trust.
- We will not engage in price fixing, predatory pricing, price gouging or "bait-and-switch" tactics.
- We will not knowingly participate in material conflicts of interest.

4. **Respect.** To acknowledge the basic human dignity of all stakeholders.

- We will value individual differences even as we avoid stereotyping customers or depicting demographic groups (e.g., gender, race, sexual orientation) in a negative or dehumanizing way in our promotions.
- We will listen to the needs of our customers and make all reasonable efforts to monitor and improve their satisfaction on an ongoing basis.

- We will make a special effort to understand suppliers, intermediaries and distributors from other cultures.
- We will appropriately acknowledge the contributions of others, such as consultants, employees and coworkers, to our marketing endeavors.

5. **Openness.** To create transparency in our marketing operations.

- We will strive to communicate clearly with all our constituencies.
- We will accept constructive criticism from our customers and other stakeholders.
- We will explain significant product or service risks, component substitutions or other foreseeable eventualities that could affect customers or their perception of the purchase decision.
- We will fully disclose list prices and terms of financing as well as available price deals and adjustments.

6. **Citizenship.** To fulfill the economic, legal, philanthropic and societal responsibilities that serve stakeholders in a strategic manner.

- We will strive to protect the natural environment in the execution of marketing campaigns.
- We will give back to the community through volunteerism and charitable donations.
- We will work to contribute to the overall betterment of marketing and its reputation.

- We will encourage supply chain members to ensure that trade is fair for all participants, including producers in developing countries.

Implementation

Finally, we recognize that every industry sector and marketing sub-discipline (e.g., marketing research, e-commerce, direct selling, direct marketing, advertising) has its own specific ethical issues that require policies and commentary. An array of such codes can be accessed through links on the AMA Web site. We encourage all such groups to develop and/or refine their industry and discipline-specific codes of ethics to supplement these general norms and values.

Unscrupulous businesspeople may receive media attention (as well as serious punishment) for their misdeeds, but fortunately their activities are usually short-lived. These people are the ones who give business a bad name and whose memory lingers with the public. The overwhelming majority of marketers, however, conduct themselves and their businesses in accordance with the tenets of the code of ethics to the mutual benefit of producer and customer.

5

REAL MARKETING PEOPLE

MAKING A CAREER decision involves many different sources of information. One way to learn more about a career path, or to consider whether a job opportunity is the right one for you, is to speak to real marketing people. Use your network of family, friends, and acquaintances to help you make informed career decisions. The interviews in this section will help you get started. We spoke to a variety of individuals who are at different levels and in various types of marketing careers. Each one has provided information about why he or she chose a particular field and what background and qualifications potential employers look for. We hope you will enjoy visiting with these talented and experienced marketers.

Promotion

The director of marketing for a regional symphony orchestra in New England, Paul Zastrow entered the field with a marketing background. He also studied music and played the trumpet. When it came to making career choices, Paul realized that he did not have the talent to be a full-time professional musician. But he was able to use that knowledge to work in a field that he really loved.

Paul's responsibilities at the orchestra include the season brochure, print and radio ads, the subscriber newsletter, and public and media relations. He also oversees box office services and the telemarketing operation.

Paul credits his ability to successfully fulfill the variety of projects for which he is responsible to his experiences in high school and college. His ability to write came not only from his classes, but also from his extracurricular activities, including editorial positions on the yearbook and the newspaper. There he also learned design techniques and people skills and developed his managerial ability.

Another important element of Paul's job is creativity. He says that it's important to learn to "think outside the box" and not become locked into your own ideas. Broad exposure to all kinds of marketing programs has helped him to develop effective ideas for marketing the symphony orchestra. Paul often borrows promotional ideas from sports as well as consumer products.

Paul believes that it is important when working in this field to market something that you believe in. He suggests that you must have a passion for what you do—if not, your life will be much less fulfilling.

Advertising (Large International Agency)

Julie Lister is an account manager at a large international advertising agency based in New York. She has worked in the industry for some sixteen years. Her interest in the field of advertising developed quite by accident. In college she started out as a biology major but switched to English literature. She also pursued her interest in the visual arts through film and photography.

Upon graduating with a liberal arts degree, Julie had to decide on a career path. Her interest in the visual arts pointed her in the direction of the production side of advertising. Through networking she landed a job with an account team for a large international client. Julie began by doing grunt work, but it gave her a chance to try out the field and to learn as much as possible about advertising. She worked hard and earned the respect of the firm's management, which eventually led to promotions and increased responsibility.

Julie notes that advertising is an intense and tough business. She urges interested students to be persistent and attentive to opportunities and follow up with hard work. That, she says, is a recipe for success in the field.

Advertising (Regional Agency)

Tracy Hogan is a senior account executive at an advertising agency based in New England that is well known for its successful retail advertising programs. Her interest in the field of advertising began as a child watching TV and being fascinated by commercials.

After earning a business degree from a four-year college, Tracy began her career selling newspaper advertising space, a job that enabled her to get a foot in the door of a field in which she really wanted to work. However, even in high school, Tracy positioned herself to work in advertising. She took advantage of a career internship opportunity that enabled her to work in an advertising agency one day per week for an entire year. She did mostly low-level work, but she also was able to accompany the account executives to TV shoots, radio recording sessions, and client meetings.

Tracy also had internships during college, during which she learned about the many facets of marketing. She advises students to pursue internships as she did, to help them make career choices as well as to learn valuable job skills and real world experience. In today's competitive job market, Tracy says that having a degree is not enough, and that any experience in a related field will give you an edge in landing the job you want.

Marketing Research

Eliot Hartstone is president of his own marketing research firm. His responsibilities range from business development to design and implementation of research projects for clients. With a bachelor's, master's, and a doctorate in sociology, Eliot's earliest plans were to enter the field of academia, and he did do some teaching while working on his doctorate. A call from the state of New York to conduct field research on violent and mentally disturbed kids in the Bronx steered Eliot into ten years of social research and teaching. Frustrations of working with the government made him switch from public to private research, specifically marketing research, and he started his own company in 1986.

Eliot believes the key influencers in his life have been his fellow researchers and their dedicated approach to their work. When assessing a potential employee, Eliot looks for effective research skills. But he also believes that strong interpersonal skills and a good work ethic are equally important factors for consideration. An employee who has a strong motivation for work will display long-term commitment to the prospective employer.

Health Care Marketing

Erik Wexler is vice president of community affairs for a large hospital in southern New England. Erik oversees all external affairs for the hospital, including fund-raising, marketing, advertising, and media relations. A combination of a bachelor's degree in sociology and an M.B.A. in marketing and management prepared him well for his current responsibilities.

Erik started his career with a graduate internship in his university's development office, where he was involved in fund-raising activities. He later became the director of development at the university. Erik cites his period of internship and the then-president of the university, Steven Trachtenberg, as key influencers in his career. Erik learned a lot from Trachtenberg, whom he considers to be "a super fund-raiser."

Together, Erik and Steve designed the university's internship program, which is currently in place. Sheer hard work and complete dedication are factors responsible for what Erik is today—a relatively young vice president servicing some sixteen hundred employees and managing a $100 million budget—and he looks for the same qualities when recruiting candidates for jobs. He considers effective oral and written communication skills to be sure selling points, in addition to organizational skills, including time management. Educational qualifications are important, but he also looks for expertise in, and commitment to, the candidate's field of work, which is demonstrated by voluntary work and internships in a chosen field.

Sales

From selling cars to selling office supplies and equipment, Jack Levine's sales career spans more than twenty years. Currently Jack is an account representative with a business equipment dealer and is responsible for five towns. He develops past, present, and future customer accounts, selling new products and service contracts to them. Jack has an associate's degree in business administration and a technical degree in design.

Jack's high school and college jobs were in sales, and he considers his grandmother to be a key influencer in not only his choice of a career, but also in how he conducts himself as a salesperson. Jack's grandmother was part owner of a car dealership, and one of the things that struck Jack about her was her ability to listen to customers and communicate with them.

From the mid 1970s to the late 1980s, Jack worked in automobile sales in various management positions. But when the bottom fell out of the industry, he opted for a change. Besides, he was no longer enjoying what he did. In 1991 he answered an advertisement for his current job and landed it.

Jack says that if he had to do it all over again he would stay in sales but would specialize in a particular area. He believes that it is a buyer's market out there. According to Jack, recruiters in sales look for sales specialists, such as in computer sales or industrial chemicals, for example, versus general salespeople. His advice to students is to concentrate in a field of study that is of interest to them and is one that they enjoy, as opposed to one that will earn them more money.

If he had to recruit a salesperson, Jack would consider the candidate's power of listening as a strong point. Listening means not just absorbing what you hear but also reading between the lines.

The customer's body language tells its own story, and keen observation skills help in identifying key signs. The other point Jack looks for is "salability"—that is, the ability to sell yourself to the client before you sell the product. The first step to this skill is in presenting yourself effectively. He also looks for the ability to build long-term relationships.

Retail

Tony Chojnowski is the owner of a clothing store and a shoe store in a small New England tourist town. At age fourteen he got into retail because he needed a job. But he found that he loved the work and now, some thirty years later, he runs his own retail business. Although he didn't start out selling clothing, by age seventeen Tony knew he loved that business and wanted to learn as much as he could, both from other retailers with whom he partnered in his initial business and from the courses he took at a local community college.

Tony explains that retail is a comprehensive business. He not only deals with employees and customers but also with vendors, financial institutions, leasing agents, lawyers, and advertising agents. One of the most important aspects that makes his business successful is knowing his customers and understanding their needs and wants. When he goes to the trade shows to buy merchandise for his stores, Tony spends the first day scanning all of the available products. That evening he reviews what he saw and fine-tunes his ideas based on his customers and the new trends for the season. Then he selects the most desirable fashions at the best price.

Tony offers the following advice to students interested in pursuing a career in retail: "The hours are long but the rewards are great. Owning your own retail business enables you to be your own boss and to take total responsibility for both your successes and your failures."

Marketing Management

Larry Chiagouris is executive vice president and director of strategic planning and research with a major worldwide advertising agency. Currently he oversees the development of strategies and marketing plans on behalf of a wide variety of clients, with an emphasis on marketing communications implications. He supervises approximately thirty individuals. His educational background includes a bachelor's degree in economics, an M.B.A. in industrial psychology, an A.P.C. in marketing, and a Ph.D. in consumer behavior.

Larry selected his career path because it provided the greatest opportunity for intellectual challenge and variety, as well as the chance to be financially rewarded for performing an intellectual task. A combination of early supervisors in his career, who were strong managers with intellectual orientations, and his professors in graduate school were key influencers in his choice of a career. Larry started his career on the client side in manufacturing and then moved on to marketing, after which he worked in an advertising agency in the area of marketing research. Moving from agency to agency, he finally settled on the area of general marketing management.

Larry's advice to students is to learn how to think analytically and develop effective verbal and written communication skills. A combination of these factors and the willingness to work hard is a sure strategy for success. Larry looks for highly energetic self-starters when recruiting, and he is also interested in those who demonstrate intellectual curiosity as well as the ability to be team players.

Consulting

Dave Gordon is the managing partner of a medium-size, full-service marketing research firm located in a major Midwest city. He is involved in the design of custom research projects and programs to meet the research objectives and information needs of clients. He is also responsible for generating new business for the company. His clients include Fortune 500 companies, and his work is mainly analyzing, interpreting, reporting, and proposing marketing actions to them. His academic background includes a B.A. in marketing and an M.B.A.

Dave began his career by taking a wide range of marketing courses, and research seemed to be the best vantage point to begin, not only a career, but also to view what was going on within companies and the industry. He did not enter marketing with the thought of a career, and in fact spent two years in brand management, learning the needs of clients and customers served by research. Dave went back to research because he realized that he liked it and wanted to return. He began on the corporate side and thought he would end up there, but instead he decided to spend some time on the supplier side, learning how to deal with the corporate world. He found that he liked the supplier side more because it offered a wider range of exposure in terms of industries and products.

Dave's advice to students is not only to develop effective written, verbal, and presentation communication skills, but also to develop the ability to get one's thoughts across effectively. He believes that employers also look for strong analytical abilities.

These, he thinks, are the qualities of a good researcher, in addition to high levels of curiosity and the desire not to take anything at face value.

When asked what his organization would look for in a new employee, Dave stated that the research field is a complex one, requiring a combination of qualitative and quantitative skills, analytical insights, and curiosity. A wide range of disciplines is applied to satisfy diverse client needs, and, therefore, he looks for a wide range of backgrounds in potential recruits, including math and statistics, psychology and sociology, communications and journalism, and marketing. Again, strong communication skills are a must.

6

THE FUTURE OF
MARKETING CAREERS

THE EMPHASIS ON marketing has been steadily growing as the business and not-for-profit environment has become more competitive. As organizations seek to differentiate their products in the marketplace and customers become better informed, the need for marketing professionals expands. Organizations rely on marketers to guide new product introduction, to observe and analyze the results of an advertising campaign, to read and interpret data on product sales, and most of all to understand customers' needs and how to respond to these needs.

Unless a company can do all these things successfully, it will soon be bypassed for others that are more responsive. More sophisticated and educated than ever, customers are quick to decide whether a product is worthwhile, and the economic consequences of a product failure are great indeed. New and exciting techniques have been developed to help organizations understand the marketplace and satisfy customer needs. Computers play their role as analytical tools, making it easier than ever to conduct research and interpret large quantities of data. All of this requires an experienced marketer to make it work.

This increasing complexity and speed of marketing decisions reflects changes in the social context. No longer are most items used at home also made at home or purchased locally. Before the days of mass production and communication, a good or service was produced and consumed in small quantities in a small geographical area by a small number of customers. The producer of a good or service usually knew his or her purchasers personally, and their individual requirements could be and frequently were accommodated. These modifications were then incorporated into the entire production run as more requests were received and word-of-mouth spread the news of these improvements. Actual advertising might have taken the form of a hand-printed sign in a shop window. At this stage, the producer handled each of the four P's.

Times have changed drastically. The increasing complexity of our society and the distance between producer and customer demand greater sophistication in our application and coordination of the marketing elements of product, price, promotion, and place/distribution.

Opportunities

Marketing has also been a field that offers abundant opportunity for both women and minorities. Whether in sales, research, or product management, the emphasis is on ability, skills, and creativity. In addition, the field of marketing is one of those in which there are several positions rated as having "faster than average" and even "much faster than average" growth potential by the United States government (see the key to projected employment later in this chapter). The descriptions of jobs that follow indicate the prospects of growth in marketing positions relative to the economy in general.

• **Advertising managers.** Marketing, advertising, and public relations managers held about 700,000 jobs in 2002. Expected to grow much faster than the average in most business services industries—such as computer and data processing, and management and public relations firms—while average growth is projected in manufacturing industries overall. Median annual earnings of marketing managers in 2002 were $57,130 for advertising and promotion managers, $78,250 for advertising managers, and $75,040 for sales managers.

• **Buyers and purchasers.** Purchasers and buyers held about 527,000 jobs in 2002. Employment of purchasers and buyers is expected to increase more slowly than the average. Median annual earnings of buyers in 2002 were $59,890.

• **Education administrators.** Education administrators held about 427,000 jobs in 2002. Employment of education administrators is expected to grow about as fast as the average. Median annual earnings of education administrators in 2002 were $71,490.

• **Graphic and visual artists.** Visual artists held about 212,000 jobs in 2002. Nearly six out of ten visual artists were self-employed. Employment of visual artists is expected to grow faster than the average. Median annual earnings of graphic artists in 2002 were $36,680.

• **Industrial designers and designers.** Designers held about 52,000 jobs in 2002. Nearly four out of ten were self-employed, compared to fewer than one out of ten workers in all occupations. Despite projected faster-than-average employment growth, designers in most fields—with the exception of floral and furniture design—are expected to face competition for available positions because many talented individuals are attracted to careers as designers. Median annual earnings of industrial designers in 2002 were $52,260.

• **Insurance agents/brokers.** Insurance agents and brokers held about 381,000 jobs in 2002. Employment of insurance agents and brokers is expected to grow more slowly than average. Median annual earnings of insurance agents in 2002 were $40,750.

• **Manufacturers' and wholesale sales representatives.** Manufacturers' and wholesale sales representatives held about 1.9 million jobs in 2002. Overall, employment of manufacturers' and wholesale sales representatives is expected to grow about as fast as the average for all occupations through the year 2006 due to continued growth in the amount of goods provided that need to be sold. Median annual earnings of manufacturers' and wholesale sales representatives in 2002 were $55,740.

• **Marketing research analysts.** Economists and marketing research analysts held about 135,000 jobs in 2002. Employment of economists and marketing research analysts is expected to grow about as fast as the average. Median annual earnings of market research analysts in 2002 were $53,810.

• **Public relations specialists.** Public relations specialists held about 158,000 jobs in 2002. Employment of public relations specialists is expected to increase faster than the average. Median annual earnings of public relations specialists in 2002 were $41,710.

• **Real estate agents.** Real estate agents, brokers, and appraisers held about 408,000 jobs in 2002. Many worked part-time, combining their real estate activities with other careers. Most real estate agents and brokers were self-employed and working on a commission basis. Employment of real estate agents, brokers, and appraisers is expected to grow more slowly than the average. Median annual earnings of real estate agents in 2002 were $30,930; for real estate brokers earnings were $50,330.

• **Retail sales worker supervisors and managers.** Retail sales worker supervisors and managers who work in retail trade held about 2.4 million wage and salary jobs in 2002. Employment of wage and salary retail sales worker supervisors and managers is expected to grow more slowly than the average. Median annual earnings of retail sales worker supervisors and managers in 2002 were $29,700.

• **Securities and financial services sales representatives.** Securities and financial services sales representatives held 300,000 jobs in 2002; securities sales representatives accounted for eight out of ten jobs. Employment of securities sales representatives is expected to grow much faster than the average. Median annual earnings of securities and financial services sales representatives in 2002 were $60,990.

Key to Projected Employment Changes Between 2002 and 2012

Grow much faster than the average—increase of 36 percent or more

Grow faster than the average—increase of 21 to 35 percent

Grow about as fast as the average—increase of 10 to 20 percent

Grow more slowly than the average, or little or no
change—increase of 3 to 9 percent
Decline—decrease of 1 percent or more

Rewards of Marketing

One of the best ways to find out what people like about their jobs
is to ask them. Talk to everyone you know who is in the field—and
even a few people you don't know (see Appendix B for a list of professional organizations that you can contact for more information).
An effective way to approach people in a position you'd like to
know more about is simply to call or write, indicating your interest
in pursuing a job in their field and asking for a few minutes to ask
their advice (at their convenience, of course). Set up an appoint-
ment to discuss their job, how they got started, features of the job,
and what course you might follow to attain a similar position. Read
some of the articles in recent publications to learn current practices
and recent developments, issues, and trends related to the field.
Sales and Marketing Management, Marketing and Media Decisions,
the marketing news section of the *New York Times,* as well as the
marketing or business sections in *Time* and *Newsweek* will all lend
background to your investigation. *Business Week*'s "Careers" section
is also a good source of information for the undergraduate or recent
graduate.

Financial Rewards

Surely the most common question about a job is "What kind of
money can I make?" Naturally there are great variations from one
region to another, even between companies, making it difficult to
present an accurate picture of potential earnings. However, we

spoke to marketing people in many different positions and in different parts of the country to verify published figures, and we compiled the following ranges for marketers with experience in Table 6.1. Of course, entry-level salaries will be much lower (as they are in any field), but chances for advancement in marketing are good. You should be able to increase your earnings and gain experience during your first few years, which will make you both promotable and marketable. Here are the findings of our salary research. Remember that they are approximate, but they should give you an idea of the ranges you can expect.

Intrinsic and Emotional Rewards

The intangible rewards that come from solving problems and serving customers often override the financial aspects. If you feel good about your work and can recognize the positive impact you can have on the products and services offered to the consuming public, you will have something money alone cannot buy. All too often we get caught up in the idea that a bigger salary, house, or car are the only rewards of a career. Personal growth, professional development, and positive feelings about one's career are frequently missing, even from those who would seem to have it all. Marketing is a field that lends itself to intrinsic rewards, as well as financial ones. It is what you make of it, so make the most of it!

Table 6.1 Marketing Career Opportunities

Marketing Career Path	Highest Degree Recommended	Technology Skills	Typical Courses Taken	Entry-Level Position	Approximate Starting Salary
Advertising	Bachelor's degree in liberal arts, advertising, or journalism; M.B.A. for account executive roles	Word processing, database applications, Adobe, Photoshop, Microsoft Office, Illustrator	Marketing, consumer behavior, sales, market research, art history, communications, photography	Administrative assistant	$25,000–$31,000
Selling	High school diploma, college degree preferred	M.S. Office, Internet skills, SFE (sales force effectiveness tools), sales portals, SFA (sales force automation)	Communications, direct selling, sales promotion	Sales assistant, entry-level job in direct selling	$28,000
Retail	Bachelor's degree Graduate degree	Inventory software, planning software, point of sale technology, intelligent vending, sign 'n' go	Merchandising, finance, inventory control, public relations	Management trainee Assistant buyer, merchandiser	$36,000–$40,000 $50,000
Communications	Bachelor's degree	Computer-aided design software, Internet skills, Adobe, Photoshop, Microsoft Office, Illustrator	Journalism, advertising, finance, political science, business administration	Communications associate, marketing and sales management trainee	$25,000–$36,000

Career	Degree required	Technical skills	Coursework	Entry-level jobs	Salary
Market research	Bachelor's degree	SPSS, SAS, modeling, Web search, statistical analysis	Marketing, statistics, communications, economics, psychology, sampling theory, sociology	Research assistant, administrative trainee, salesperson, marketing interviewer	$30,000
	Master's or doctorate			Analyst, statistician	$33,000–$38,000
Marketing management	M.B.A.	Website development, Powerpoint, Excel	Marketing, buyer behavior, marketing policy, advertising, industrial marketing, sales management, international marketing, personal selling	Marketing associate, entry-level job in import-export firms	$30,000–$38,000
Product management	M.B.A., master's degree in economics	Interaction design skills, HTML designing, user-centered design, UI wire frames, visual design, project management software	Product development and management, marketing finance, marketing strategy	Product/brand manager	$40,000–$50,000
Health care marketing	Master's degree in health service administration	Microsoft Office, sales tracking software, Quark, InDesign	Health care marketing and strategy, leadership in health care organizations, health finance and economics	Medical equipment sales and purchase representative	$25,000–$36,400

(continued)

Table 6.1 Marketing Career Opportunities (*continued*)

Marketing Career Path	Highest Degree Recommended	Technology Skills	Typical Courses Taken	Entry-Level Position	Approximate Starting Salary
Consulting	Bachelor's degree, on-the-job training, M.B.A.	Analytical problem solving	Business, management marketing, accounts, economics, leadership, computers	Management analyst	$40,000–$80,000
E-business marketing	Bachelor's degree and e-commerce certificate or diploma	Web searching, data mining and visualization, distributed computing applications, networking, Web services, semantic Web, computer vision and image processing	Sales strategy, e-business and communications, innovation and entrepreneurship, conducting business electronically, telecommunications and media law	Web page designer, systems analyst, database manager, database developer, network analyst	$35,000–$100,000
Customer service	High school diploma, college degree preferred	E-mail, basic computer skills, good typing skills	Computers, English, business, foreign language	Customer care representative, customer service associate	$20,000–$40,000

Sources: University of Technology Sydney, ExecutiveAudioInstitute.com, Inc.com, Salary.com, Jobweb.com, Seneca Career Resources, CareerBuilder.com, CareerNet.com, Monster.com, Stores.org, U.S Department of Labor, hotjobs.com, vault.com, JobHunt.com, WetFeet.com, Careers-in-business.com, Marketingjobs.com.

7

MARKET YOURSELF

Now THAT YOU'VE learned about marketing in general, it's time to apply some marketing techniques to yourself—the college applicant or job seeker. Yes, the four Ps can be put to work by you and for you, so just sit back and we'll tell you how.

Your Product

First, think of yourself as a product (the first "P"). Who are your customers? Aren't they the people who will be judging your entrance essay or your résumé? Of course they are, and like any good marketer your first step is to get to know them (personally or not) and find out what it is they want in this kind of product—a student or employee. Reread the comments made by the marketers in Chapter 5 for some ideas of what makes a job applicant look promising. Talk to people who are now students at the school you would like to attend, and ask them what kind of person fits in best. You may find out in the process that a particular school or job is not right for you, but that is one of the purposes of this exercise.

As you learn about what employers look for, think about what you are looking for in an employer and how the two might or might not fit together. This goes for schools, too, as what one student likes about the diversity of a large university, for example, another may find distracting or confusing. Do some marketing research and dig up all you can about your target customer.

If you are looking for a job in a particular field, you can do a Google search relating to that field, as well as search the sites of local and national news media for pieces on specific companies. The trade journals and websites of any given field will give you even greater depth of information.

For an overall financial picture, the 10-K published by the Securities Exchange Commission is invaluable and should be used as a balance to the annual report put out by a company. This kind of research is called doing your homework for an interview, and it will help you speak intelligently to a recruiter or personnel representative. By taking the time and effort to do this research, you demonstrate your interest in a field and company in addition to your commitment to obtaining meaningful and rewarding work.

Your Price

The price, of course, is your salary. Naturally you want the highest you can obtain, but isn't there more to rewarding work than just money? Take this into account as you weigh different opportunities. Don't overlook the experience you might gain as part of the compensation for a career position.

Your Place

You must also be in the right place at the right time. Only you have your unique set of skills, and one of these skills is convincing a potential employer that you are the one right person for that job. They need someone like you right now, and here you are!

Your Promotion

Promotion is the fourth "P." You are sending out résumés, following up, talking to anyone and everyone, establishing contacts, making connections, all with your potential customers. Doesn't that qualify as self-promotion? Of course it does, and it works very well indeed. You obtained professional assistance with your résumé and cover letter and learned how to best present your prior experience, academic credentials, and career objectives. Now that your paper self is professional, what about your personal self? Is it professional, too?

We hope we don't need to remind you to dress neatly and conservatively for your interview. That does not mean you must run out and buy a three-piece navy suit, but your interview attire should be professional. Suits are still the overwhelming favorite, and it's hard to go wrong with one. Remember, you will be judged by the appearance you present, and first impressions are the ones that will be remembered most. Take advantage of this and put your best foot (shoes shined!) forward. Not only will you look better, you'll feel better—more comfortable and confident. Even though you may be wearing a suit and the appropriate accessories, your comfort will be based on being appropriately and professionally dressed.

Career-Related Websites

The websites listed here are devoted to finding jobs. Check some of them out.

CareerBuilder.com
CareerNet.com
JobHunt.com
Marketingjobs.com
Monster.com
Salary.com
WetFeet.com
Yahoo HotJobs.com

Interview Questions and Self-Assessment

This is a collection of some of the most frequently used questions on job interviews. You can develop your answers to these in the course of analyzing your career goals and your professional needs. Use these questions and comments as a guide to your self-analysis, and review your answers throughout the course of your career (academic, business, or both).

- What are your long-range career objectives? In other words, what are you looking for from a career besides the obvious ability to pay the bills?
- How do you plan to accomplish these objectives? What are you doing to work toward your goals? Are you continuing your education or applying yourself wholeheartedly to your current position?

- Why did you select this career? Are you really committed to this line of work or did it just sound glamorous? Is it really a career for you?
- What do you see yourself doing in five years? In ten years? This is a corollary to your long-range career goals, but with specific deadlines.
- What nonoccupational goals have you set for yourself over the next ten years? What is your personal agenda?
- What do you really want to do in life? Be careful, if the answer is not the career you are applying for, something is amiss and needs attention.
- What are the most important rewards you expect from your career? Is money the only thing that you want from your job? There are other paybacks that are frequently more satisfying than money.
- What salary do you think you will earn in five years? How realistic are your goals? How ambitious are you?
- Which is more important to you, the kind of work you do or the salary? Again, how money oriented are you? Your employer wants a well-rounded worker, one who seeks satisfaction in doing a good job.
- How has your college experience prepared you for a career in business? What did you learn besides your academic area? Did you gain any interpersonal and communication skills or were you a loner?
- What qualifications do you have that you think will make you successful in business? Are you organized, a team player, a good communicator, a leader?
- What does success mean to you? Is it a large salary, corporate power, an expensive car, or job satisfaction?

- What do you think it takes to be successful in this kind of organization? Do you expect ruthless competitiveness or the cooperation of working toward a common goal?
- How do you think you can contribute to this firm? What skills and attitude do you have? Will you be a thoughtful, productive team member?
- Why should I hire you? This is important. Emphasize that you would be the perfect employee—that this job has your name on it. Play up your skills and turn your weaknesses into learning opportunities.
- How would you describe yourself? Use a few well-chosen words, like intelligent, curious, cooperative—you get the idea.
- How do you think a friend or professor who knows you well would describe you? Again, only a few words are necessary. Industrious, diligent, and so forth.
- What motivates you to work your hardest? What makes you really tick, and is it something the organization does already? Or are you going to be someone the organization has to light a fire under?
- What accomplishments have given you the most satisfaction? Why? The answer to this question yields several clues to what you've done, as well as what you like to do.
- What was your most rewarding experience in college? How did you utilize your college years to gain the most from them? Naturally you'd want to mention the community service award you received, not the night you went on a bender with your buddies.
- Why did you choose the school you attended? How selective were you? How choosy was the school? Did you take an active part?

- How did you select your major? How well researched was your decision? Again, did you take an active role?
- What subjects did you enjoy most? Why? Of course, your major should be high on this list, but what about others outside your discipline? You want to stress that you are a well-rounded individual.
- If you could do it again, what would you change in your college studies? Ah, the famous hindsight question, which demands a thoughtful answer. Do not treat this one lightly.
- What changes would you make in your college? Given the chance, how would you improve your school academically?
- Do you plan to continue your education? What kind of degree would you pursue? How does it relate to your career? Indicate some consideration of an advanced degree or additional training.
- What did you learn from participating in extracurricular activities? How did you develop personally? Can you work with or lead others?
- If you were looking for someone to fill this position, what kind of person would you hire? Someone just like yourself, of course—bright, articulate, well-versed in the field.
- How are you evaluating organizations you might like to work for? Preferably not just by salary or proximity to the beach. Opportunity for advancement and professional growth should rate high on the list.
- What made you decide to apply to this organization? It would certainly be helpful to stress the professional opportunities offered by the firm as well as its reputation as a leader in its field.
- In what kind of work are you most at home? Are you quantitatively oriented and happy with numbers, or do

figures make you run the other way but you're terrific with people?

- Describe your ideal job. Challenging, yes, but in what way? Opportunity for growth and advancement should figure in this answer.
- How do you work under pressure? Are you cool, calm, and collected, or do you yell at people but still get the job done? Should you consider another line of work?
- What qualities do you think make a good manager? This is really asking about what kinds of people you work best with; in other words, who are you most compatible with?
- What kind of manager/subordinate relationship do you think works best? What has your interpersonal experience been and will it fit in with the organization?
- What size organization do you want to work for? This also relates to your interpersonal style and experience, along with the organizational differences between large and small companies. What are your reasons behind your preference?
- How do you analyze potential employers? Are you looking for a large, well-established organization with a deeply entrenched political structure, or are you entrepreneurial and a risk taker looking for a more flexible structure?
- Why did you leave a previous job? A desire for professional advancement and/or a better opportunity should figure in your answer.
- Will you relocate? Do you prefer a specific geographical area? Why? Will you travel? How flexible are you, and how much do you want that promotion? In some organizations mobility is the key to advancement, and willingness is taken for granted.

- What have you learned from your mistakes? How have you turned blunders into learning opportunities? Or are you going to continue to make the same errors over and over?
- Are you a perfectionist? A favorite loaded question, this one requires a careful answer. If you say "yes," do you mean you cannot tolerate any coworkers' foibles? If you say "no," does it indicate lower standards for your own work? Watch this one!

We've just about exhausted popular interview territory. Take a few minutes every so often to think about these questions and further develop your answers. Not only will you be better prepared for the interview, but you also will have gained insight to your own career requirements.

Colleges with Majors in Marketing, Distribution, Distributive Education, Retailing, and Merchandising

THE FOUR-YEAR COLLEGES in this appendix offer majors in marketing and related courses of study. For more information and the addresses for the schools you're interested in, refer to *Profiles of American Colleges*, Barron's Educational Series; *Peterson's Guide to Graduate Programs in Business, Education, Health, Information Studies, Law, and Social Work*; and the *Marketing News International Directory* of the American Marketing Association. Address your correspondence to the department of marketing of each school in which you are interested.

Information is also available on the following Web pages.

U.S. Department of Education
600 Independence Ave. SW
Washington, DC 20202-0498
(800) USA-LEARN
www.ed.gov

Federal Student Aid Information Center
(800) 4-FED-AID (800-433-3243)
www.ed.gov/offices/ope

U.S. Department of Education
Office of Postsecondary Education
Regional Office Building 3 (ROB-3)
Seventh and D St.s SW
Washington, DC 20202
www.ed.gov/offices/ope/index.html

Bachelor's Degree

The following schools offer bachelor's degrees in marketing and marketing-related subjects.

Alabama

Alabama Agricultural and
Mechanical University
www.aamu.edu

Alabama State University
www.alasu.edu

Auburn University
www.auburn.edu

Birmingham–Southern
College
www.bsc.edu

Jacksonville State University
www.jsu.edu

Samford University
www.samford.edu

Spring Hill College
www.shc.edu

Troy State University–Dothan
www.tsud.edu

Troy State University–Troy
www.troyst.edu

Tuskegee University
www.tuskegee.edu

University of
 Alabama–Birmingham
www.uab.edu

University of
 Alabama–Huntsville
www.uah.edu

University of
 Alabama–Tuscaloosa
www.ua.edu

University of Mobile
www.umobile.edu

University of Montevallo
www.montevallo.edu

University of North Alabama
www.una.edu

University of South Alabama
www.southalabama.edu

University of West Alabama
www.uwa.edu

Alaska

Alaska Pacific University
www.alaskapacific.edu

University of
 Alaska–Anchorage
www.uaa.alaska.edu

Arizona

Arizona State University
www.asu.edu

Grand Canyon University
www.grand-canyon.edu

Northern Arizona University
www.nau.edu

University of Arizona
www.arizona.edu

University of Phoenix
www.uophx.edu

Western International
 University
www.wintu.edu

Arkansas

Arkansas State University
www.astate.edu

Harding University
www.harding.edu

Ouachita Baptist University
www.obu.edu

Southern Arkansas University
www.saumag.edu

University of Arkansas at
Fayetteville
www.uark.edu

University of
Arkansas–Little Rock
www.ualr.edu

University of Central
Arkansas
www.uca.edu

University of Ozarks
www.ozarks.edu

California

Azusa Pacific University
www.apu.edu

California Lutheran
University
www.clunet.edu

California State Polytech
University–Pomona
www.csupomona.edu

California State
University–Fullerton
www.fullerton.edu

California State
University–Long Beach
www.csulb.edu

California State
University–Los Angeles
www.calstatela.edu

California State
University–Northridge
www.csun.edu

California State
University–Sacramento
www.csus.edu

California State
University–San Bernardino
www.csusb.edu

College at Notre Dame
www.ndnu.edu

Golden Gate University
www.ggu.edu

La Sierra University
www.lasierra.edu

Menlo College
www.menlo.edu

Mount Saint Mary's College
www.msmc.la.edu

National University
www.nu.edu

San Francisco State University
www.sfsu.edu

San Jose State University
www.sjsu.edu

Santa Clara University
www.scu.edu

Southern California College
www.scco.edu

University of La Verne
www.ulaverne.edu

University of San Francisco
www.usfca.edu

Woodbury University
www.woodbury.edu

Colorado

Adams State College
www.adams.edu

Colorado Christian University
www.ccu.edu

Colorado State University
www.colostate.edu

Metropolitan State College
www.mscd.edu

Regis College of Regis
University
www.regis.edu

University of Denver
www.du.edu

University of Northern
Colorado
www.unco.edu

Connecticut

Central Connecticut State
University
www.ccsu.edu

Fairfield University
www.fairfield.edu

Quinnipiac College
www.quinnipiac.edu

Southern Connecticut State
University
www.southernct.edu

University of Bridgeport
www.bridgeport.edu

University of
   Connecticut–Storrs
www.uconn.edu

University of Hartford
www.hartford.edu

University of New Haven
www.newhaven.edu

Western Connecticut State
   University
www.wcsu.edu

Delaware

Delaware State University
www.dsc.edu

Goldey Beacom College
www.goldey.gbc.edu

University of Delaware
www.udel.edu

Wesley College
www.wesley.edu

District of Columbia

American University
www.american.edu

George Washington
   University
www.gwu.edu

Howard University
www.howard.edu

Southeastern University
www.seu.edu

University of the District of
   Columbia
www.universityofdc.org

Florida

Barry University
www.barry.edu

Florida Atlantic University
www.fau.edu

Florida International
   University
www.fiu.edu

Florida Metropolitan
   University–Tampa
www.fmu.edu

Florida Southern College
www.flsouthern.edu

Florida State University
www.fsu.edu

Jacksonville University
www.ju.edu

Lynn University
www.lynn.cdu

Northwood University
www.northwood.edu

Orlando College
www.herzing.edu/orlando

Palm Beach Atlantic College
www.pba.edu

Schiller International
　University–Florida
　Campus
www.schiller.edu

St. Thomas University
www.stu.edu

Stetson University
www.stetson.edu

University of Central Florida
www.ucf.edu

University of Florida
www.ufl.edu

University of Miami
www.miami.edu

University of North Florida
www.unf.edu

University of South Florida
www.usf.edu

University of Tampa
www.utampa.edu

University of West Florida
www.uwf.edu

Webber College
www.webber.edu

Georgia

Albany State College
http://asuweb.asurams.edu

Augusta State University
www.aug.edu

Clayton College and State
　University
www.clayton.edu

Columbus State University
www.colstate.edu

Emory University
www.emory.edu

Fort Valley State College
www.fvsu.edu

Georgia College and State
University
www.gcsu.edu

Georgia Southern University
www.georgiasouthern.edu

Georgia Southwestern State
University
www.gsw.edu

Georgia State University
www.gsu.edu

Kennesaw College
www.kennesaw.edu

Mercer University–Atlanta
www.mercer.edu

Morehouse College
www.morehouse.edu

North Georgia College
www.ngcsu.edu

Savannah State University
www.savstate.edu

University of West Georgia
www.westga.edu

Valdosta State University
www.valdosta.edu

Women's College of Brenau
University
www.brenau.edu

Hawaii

Chaminade University of
Honolulu
www.chaminade.edu

Hawaii Pacific University
www.hpu.edu

University of Hawaii–Manoa
www.hawaii.edu

Idaho

Boise State University
www.boisestate.edu

Idaho State University
www.isu.edu

University of Idaho
www.uidaho.edu

Illinois

Aurora University
www.aurora.edu

Benedictine University
www.ben.edu

Bradley University
www.bradley.edu

Chicago State University
www.csu.edu

DePaul University
www.depaul.edu

Eastern Illinois University
www.eiu.edu

Elmhurst College
www.elmhurst.edu

Greenville College
www.greenville.edu

Illinois State University
www.ilstu.edu

Lewis University
www.lewisu.edu

Loyola University of Chicago
www.luc.edu

MacMurray College
www.mac.edu

McKendree College
www.mckendree.edu

Millikin University
www.millikin.edu

North Central College
www.noctrl.edu

North Park College
www.northpark.edu

Northeastern Illinois
University
www.neiu.edu

Northern Illinois University
www.niu.edu

Quincy College
www.quincycollege.edu

Roosevelt University
www.roosevelt.edu

Saint Xavier College
www.sxu.edu

Southern Illinois
University–Carbondale
www.siuc.edu

Trinity Christian College
www.trnty.edu

Trinity International
University
www.tiu.edu

University of Illinois at
Chicago
www.uic.edu

University of Illinois at
Urbana–Champaign
www.uiuc.edu

University of Saint Francis
www.stfrancis.edu

Western Illinois University
www.wiu.edu

Indiana

Anderson University
www.anderson.edu

Ball State University
www.bsu.edu

Butler University
www.butler.edu

Indiana Institute of
Technology
www.indtech.edu

Indiana Wesleyan University
www.indwes.edu

Martin University
www.martin.edu

Purdue University–Calumet
www.calumet.purdue.edu

St. Mary-of-the-Woods
College
www.smwc.edu

Tri-State University
www.tristate.edu

University of Evansville
www.evansville.edu

University of Indianapolis
www.uindy.edu

University of Notre Dame
www.nd.edu

University of Southern
Indiana
www.usi.edu

Valparaiso University
www.valpo.edu

Iowa

Buena Vista University
www.bvu.edu

Clarke College
www.clarke.edu

Drake University
www.drake.edu

Grand View College
www.gvc.edu

Iowa State University
www.iastate.edu

Loras College
www.loras.edu

University of Dubuque
www.dbq.edu

University of Iowa
www.uiowa.edu

University of Northern Iowa
www.uni.edu

Upper Iowa University
www.uiu.edu

William Penn College
www.wmpenn.edu

Kansas

Emporia State University
www.emporia.edu

Fort Hays State University
www.fhsu.edu

Kansas Newman College
www.newmanu.edu

Kansas State University
www.ksu.edu

Manhattan Christian College
www.mccks.edu

Pittsburg State University
www.pittstate.edu

Washburn University of
Topeka
www.washburn.edu

Wichita State University
www.wichita.edu

Kentucky

Eastern Kentucky University
www.eku.edu

Georgetown College
www.georgetowncollege.edu

Murray State University
www.murraystate.edu

Sullivan College
www.sullivan.edu

Louisiana

Grambling State University
www.gram.edu

Louisiana State
University–Shreveport
www.lsus.edu

Loyola University
www.loyno.edu

Northeast Louisiana
University
www.ulm.edu

Southeastern Louisiana
University
www.selu.edu

Southern University–Baton
Rouge
www.subr.edu

University of New Orleans
www.uno.edu

University of Southwestern
Louisiana
www.louisiana.edu

Xavier University of Louisiana
www.xula.edu

Maine

Husson College
www.husson.edu

Saint Joseph's College
www.sjcme.edu

Thomas College
www.thomas.edu

University of Maine at
Machias
www.umm.maine.edu

University of Maine at Orono
www.umaine.edu

Maryland

College of Notre Dame of
Maryland
www.ndm.edu

Morgan State University
www.morgan.edu

University of Baltimore
www.ubalt.edu

University College
www.umuc.edu

Massachusetts

American International
College
www.aic.edu

Babson College
www.babson.edu

Boston College
www.bc.edu

Elms College
www.elms.edu

LaSalle College
www.lasalle.edu

Merrimack College
www.merrimack.edu

Nichols College
www.nichols.edu

Salem State College
www.salemstate.edu

Simmons College
www.simmons.edu

Suffolk University
www.suffolk.edu

University of
    Massachusetts–Amherst
www.umass.edu

University of
    Massachusetts–Dartmouth
www.umassd.edu

Western New England College
www.wnec.edu

Michigan

Andrews University
www.andrews.edu

Baker College
www.baker.edu

Central Michigan University
www.cmich.edu

Davenport College–Grand
    Rapids
www.davenport.edu

Davenport College–Lansing
www.davenport.edu

Eastern Michigan University
www.emich.edu

Ferris State College
www.ferris.edu

Grand Valley State University
www.gvsu.edu

Hillsdale College
www.hillsdale.edu

Madonna University
www.munet.edu

Michigan State University
www.msu.edu

Northern Michigan University
www.nmu.edu

Northwood Institute
www.wmich.edu

Oakland University
www.oakland.edu

Olivet College
www.olivetcollege.edu

Wayne State University
www.wayne.edu

Western Michigan University
www.wmich.edu

Minnesota

Augsburg College
www.augsburg.edu

Bethel University
www.bethel.edu

College of St. Catherine–
St. Catherine Campus
www.stkate.edu

Concordia College
www.cord.edu

Moorhead State University
www.mnstate.edu

Northwestern College
www.nwc.edu

Southwest State University
www.southwest.msus.edu

St. Cloud State University
www.stcloudstate.edu

University of
Minnesota–Twin Cities
www.umn.edu

Winona State University
www.winona.edu

Mississippi

Delta State University
www.deltastate.edu

Jackson State University
www.jsums.edu

Mississippi State University
www.msstate.edu

Rust College
www.rustcollege.edu

University of Mississippi
www.olemiss.edu

University of Southern
Mississippi
www.usm.edu

Missouri

Avila College
www.avila.edu

Central Missouri State
University
www.cmsu.edu

College of the Ozarks
www.cofo.edu

Evangel University
www.evangel.edu

Fontbonne College
www.fontbonne.edu

Lincoln University
www.lincolnu.edu

Missouri Southern State
University
www.mssu.edu

Missouri Valley College
www.moval.edu

Missouri Western State
College
www.mwsc.edu

Northwest Missouri State
University
www.nwmissouri.edu

Rockhurst College
www.rockhurst.edu

Southeast Missouri State
University
www.semo.edu

Southwest Missouri State
University
www.smsu.edu

St. Louis University
www.slu.edu

Truman State University
www.truman.edu

Webster University
www.webster.edu

William Woods College
www.wmwoods.edu

Montana

Montana State
University–Billings
www.msubillings.edu

University of Great Falls
www.ugf.edu

University of Montana
www.umt.edu

Nebraska

Creighton University
www.creighton.edu

Hastings College
www.hastings.edu

Peru State College
www.peru.edu

Union College
www.ucollege.edu

University of
Nebraska–Omaha
www.unomaha.edu

Nevada

Morrison College
www.morrison.northface.edu

University of
Nevada–Las Vegas
www.unlv.edu

University of Nevada–Reno
www.unr.edu

New Hampshire

Franklin Pierce College
www.fpc.edu

New Hampshire College
www.nhc.edu

Plymouth State College
www.plymouth.edu

Rivier College
www.rivier.edu

New Jersey

Bloomfield College
www.bloomfield.edu

Fairleigh Dickinson University
www.fdu.edu

Jersey City State College
www.njcu.edu

Rutgers State University–New
Brunswick
www.nbp.rutgers.edu

Rutgers State
University–Newark
www.newark.rutgers.edu

Rutgers University, Camden
College of Arts and
Sciences
www.camden.rutgers.edu

Rutgers University, Douglas
College
www.douglass.rutgers.edu

Rutgers University, Livingston
College
www.livingston.rutgers.edu

Rutgers University, Newark
Colleges of Arts and
Sciences
www.newark.rutgers.edu

Rutgers University, Rutgers
College
www.rutgerscollege.rutgers.edu

Rutgers University, University
College Camden
www.camden.rutgers.edu

St. Peter's College
www.spc.edu

Thomas Edison State College
www.tesc.edu

New Mexico

College of the Southwest
www.csw.edu

Eastern New Mexico
University
www.enmu.edu

New Mexico Highlands
University
www.nmhu.edu

New Mexico State University
www.nmsu.edu

University of New Mexico
www.unm.edu

Western New Mexico
University
www.wnmu.edu

New York

Canisius College
www.canisius.edu

City University of New York
www.cuny.edu

Clarkson University
www.clarkson.edu

CUNY-Bernard M. Baruch
College
www.baruch.cuny.edu

CUNY-York College
www.york.cuny.edu

Dominican College
www.dc.edu

Dowling College
www.dowling.edu

Elmira College
www.elmira.edu

Iona College
www.iona.edu

Ithaca College
www.ithaca.edu

Keuka College
www.keuka.edu

Long Island University,
C. W. Post Campus
www.cwpost.liu.edu

New York University
www.nyu.edu

Niagara University
www.niagara.edu

Pace University–New York
www.pace.edu

Pace University–Pleasantville
www.pace.edu

Parsons School of Design
www.parsons.edu

Rochester Institute of
Technology
www.rit.edu

Saint John's University
www.stjohns.edu

St. Joseph's College
www.sjcny.edu

Siena College
www.siena.edu

St. Bonaventure University
www.sbu.edu

St. Thomas Aquinas College
www.stac.edu

State University of New York,
College at Oswego
www.oswego.edu

Syracuse University
www.syr.edu

Touro College
www.touro.edu

University of the State of New York
www.suny.edu

North Carolina

Appalachian State University
www.acs.appstate.edu

Barber-Scotia College
www.b-sc.edu

Barton College
www.barton.edu

East Carolina University
www.ecu.edu

Fayetteville State University
www.uncfsu.edu

Pfeiffer College
www.pfeiffer.edu

University of North Carolina–Greensboro
www.uncg.edu

University of North Carolina–Wilmington
www.uncw.edu

Western Carolina University
www.wcu.edu

North Dakota

University of North Dakota–Grand Forks
www.und.edu

Ohio

Ashland University
www.ashland.edu

Baldwin-Wallace College
www.bw.edu

Bowling Green State University
www.bgsu.edu

Cedarville College
www.cedarville.edu

Central State University
www.centralstate.edu

David N. Myers College
www.dnmyers.edu

Defiance College
www.defiance.edu

John Carroll University
www.jcu.edu

Kent State University
www.kent.edu

Marietta College
www.marietta.edu

Miami University–Oxford
www.muohio.edu

Mount Union College
www.muc.edu

Notre Dame College of Ohio
www.ndc.edu

Ohio State
    University–Columbus
www.osu.edu

Ohio University–Athens
www.ohiou.edu

Otterbein College
www.otterbein.edu

Tiffin University
www.tiffin.edu

University of Cincinnati
www.uc.edu

University of Dayton
www.udayton.edu

University of Findlay
www.findlay.edu

University of Rio Grande
www.urgrgcc.edu

University of Toledo
www.utoledo.edu

Walsh University
www.walsh.edu

Wilberforce University
www.wilberforce.edu

Wilmington College
www.wilmcoll.edu

Wittenberg University
www.wittenberg.edu

Wright State University
www.wright.edu

Xavier University
www.xu.edu

Youngstown State University
www.ysu.edu

Oklahoma

East Central University
www.ecok.edu

Northeastern State University
www.nsuok.edu

Oklahoma Baptist University
www.okbu.edu

Oklahoma Christian College
www.oc.edu

Oklahoma City University
www.okcu.edu

Oral Roberts University
www.oru.edu

Southeastern Oklahoma State
University
www.sosu.edu

Southwestern Oklahoma State
University
www.swosu.edu

University of Central
Oklahoma
www.ucok.edu

University of Science and Arts
www.usao.edu

University of Tulsa
www.utulsa.edu

Oregon

Northwest Christian College
www.nwcc.edu

Oregon State University
www.oregonstate.edu

Portland State University
www.pdx.edu

University of Portland
www.up.edu

Pennsylvania

Allentown College of Saint
Francis de Sales
www.desales.edu

Cabrini College
www.cabrini.edu

California University of
Pennsylvania
www.cup.edu

Carnegie Mellon University
www.cmu.edu

Clarion University of
Pennsylvania
www.clarion.edu

College of Misericordia
www.misericordia.edu

Delaware Valley College
www.devalcol.edu

Drexel University
www.drexel.edu

Duquesne University
www.duq.edu

Edinboro University of
Pennsylvania
www.edinboro.edu

Gannon University
www.gannon.edu

Geneva College
www.geneva.edu

Grove City College
www.gcc.edu

Holy Family College
www.hfc.edu

Indiana University of
Pennsylvania
www.iup.edu

Juniata College
www.juniata.edu

King's College
www.kings.edu

La Salle University
www.lasalle.edu

Marywood College
www.marywood.edu

Messiah College
www.messiah.edu

Millersville University of
Pennsylvania
www.muweb.millersville.edu

Philadelphia University
www.philau.edu

Seton Hill College
www.setonhill.edu

Shippensburg University of
Pennsylvania
www.ship.edu

Slippery Rock University
www.sru.edu

St. Joseph's University
www.sju.edu

Susquehanna University
www.susqu.edu

Temple University
www.temple.edu

University of Pennsylvania
www.upenn.edu

University of Scranton
www.scranton.edu

Villanova University
www.villanova.edu

Waynesburg College
www.waynesburg.edu

West Chester University of
Pennsylvania
www.wcupa.edu

York College of Pennsylvania
www.ycp.edu

Puerto Rico

Bayamon Central University
www.ucb.edu

Bayamon Technological
University
www.ucb.edu.pr

Caribbean University
www.caribbean.edu

Inter American University of
Puerto Rico–Aguadilla
www.interaguadilla.edu

Inter American University of
Puerto Rico–Bayamon
University College
www.bc.inter.edu

Inter American University of
Puerto Rico–Fajardo
Regional College
www.fajardo.inter.edu

Inter American University of
Puerto Rico–Metropolitan
Campus
www.metro.inter.edu

Inter American University of
Puerto Rico–Ponce
Regional College
www.ponce.inter.edu

Inter American University of
Puerto Rico–San German
www.sg.inter.edu

Pontifical Catholic University
www.pucpr.edu

Turabo University
www.suagm.edu

University of Puerto
Rico–Mayaguez
www.uprm.edu

University of Puerto
Rico–Rio Piedras
www.rrp.upr.edu

University of the Sacred Heart
www.sacredheart.edu

Rhode Island

Bryant College
www.bryant.edu

Johnson & Wales University
www.jwu.edu

Providence College
www.providence.edu

Rhode Island College
www.ric.edu

Roger Williams
University–Bristol
www.rwu.edu

University of Rhode Island
www.uri.edu

South Carolina

Benedict College
www.benedict.edu

Bob Jones University
www.bju.edu

Charleston Southern
University
www.csuniv.edu

Claflin College
www.claflin.edu

Coker College
www.coker.edu

Clemson University
www.clemson.edu

Limestone College
www.limestone.edu

South Carolina State College
www.scsu.edu

University of South Carolina
www.sc.edu

University of South
Carolina–Aiken
www.usca.edu

South Dakota

Dakota State University
www.dsu.edu

Northern State University
www.northern.edu

Tennessee

Austin Peay State University
www.apsu.edu

Belmont University
www.belmont.edu

Christian Brothers University
www.cbu.edu

Cumberland University
www.cumberland.edu

East Tennessee State
University
www.etsu.edu

Freed Hardeman University
www.fhu.edu

Lambuth University
·www.lambuth.edu

Lincoln Memorial University
www.lmunet.edu

Middle Tennessee State
University
www.mtsu.edu

Southern Adventists
University
www.southern.edu

Tennessee Tech University
www.tntech.edu

Union University
www.uu.edu

University of Memphis
www.memphis.edu

University of
Tennessee–Knoxville
www.utk.edu

University of
Tennessee–Martin
www.utm.edu

Texas

Abilene Christian University
www.acu.edu

Amberton University
www.amberton.edu

Angelo State University
www.angelo.edu

Baylor University
www.baylor.edu

Dallas Baptist University
www.dbu.edu

East Texas State University
www.etsu.edu

Hardin-Simmons University
www.hsutx.edu

Houston Baptist University
www.hbu.edu

Howard Payne University
www.hputx.edu

Huston-Tillotson College
www.htc.edu

Jarvis Christian College
www.jarvis.edu

Le Tourneau University
www.letu.edu

McMurry University
www.mcm.edu

Midwestern State University
www.mwsu.edu

Prairie View A & M
   University
www.pvamu.edu

Sam Houston State University
www.shsu.edu

Southwest Texas State
   University
www.swt.edu

St. Mary's University
www.stmarytx.edu

Stephen F. Austin State
   University
www.sfasu.edu

Tarleton State University
www.tarleton.edu

Texas A & M International
   University
www.tamiu.edu

Texas A & M
   University–Main Campus
www.tamu.edu

Texas A & M
   University–Commerce
www.tamu-commerce.edu

Texas A & M
   University–Kingsville
www.tamuk.edu

Texas Southern University
www.tsu.edu

Texas Tech University
www.ttu.edu

Texas Wesleyan University
www.txwes.edu

University of
Houston–Clear Lake
www.cl.uh.edu

University of
Houston–University Park
www.uh.edu

University of Incarnate Word
www.uiw.edu

University of North Texas
www.unt.edu

University of Texas–El Paso
www.utep.edu

University of
Texas–Pan American
www.panam.edu

University of Texas of
Permian Basin
www.utpb.edu

University of
Texas–San Antonio
www.utsa.edu

West Texas A & M University
www.wtamu.edu

Utah

Brigham Young Texas
University
www.byu.edu

University of Utah
www.utah.edu

Utah State University
www.usu.edu

Weber State University
www.weber.edu

Vermont

Castleton State College
www.csc.vsc.edu

Champlain College
www.champlain.edu

Virginia

Averett College
www.averett.edu

Christopher Newport
University
www.cnu.edu

Hampton University
www.hamptonu.edu

James Madison University
www.jmu.edu

Marymount University
www.marymount.edu

Old Dominion University
www.odu.edu

Radford University
www.radford.edu

Virginia Commonwealth
University
www.vcu.edu

Virginia Intermont College
www.vic.edu

Virginia Tech University
www.vt.edu

Virginia Wesleyan University
www.vwc.edu

West Virginia State University
www.wvsc.edu

Washington

Central Washington University
www.cwu.edu

City University
www.cityu.edu

Eastern Washington
University
www.ewu.edu

Pacific Lutheran University
www.plu.edu

Seattle University
www.seattleu.edu

Walla Walla College
www.wwc.edu

Washington State University
www.wsu.edu

West Virginia

Davis and Elkins College
www.davisandelkins.edu

Fairmont State
www.fscwv.edu

Glennville State College
www.glenville.wvnet.edu

Marshall University
www.marshall.edu

Salem International University
www.salemiu.edu

Shepherd College
www.shepherd.edu

University of Charleston
www.uchaswv.edu

West Virginia State College
www.wvsc.edu

West Virginia Wesleyan
College
www.wvwc.edu

Wheeling Jesuit College
www.wju.edu

Wisconsin

Carthage College
www.carthage.edu

Lakeland College
www.lakeland.edu

Marian College of Fond
du Lac
www.mariancoll.edu

Marquette University
www.marquette.edu

University of
Wisconsin–Eau Claire
www.uwec.edu

University of
Wisconsin–Madison
www.wisc.edu

University of
Wisconsin–Milwaukee
www.uwm.edu

University of
Wisconsin–Oshkosh
www.uwosh.edu

University of
Wisconsin–Superior
www.uwsuper.edu

University of
Wisconsin–Whitewater
www.uww.edu

Viterbo College
www.viterbo.edu

Wyoming

University of Wyoming
www.uwyo.edu

Master's Degree

The following schools offer master's degrees in marketing and marketing-related subjects.

Alabama

Alabama State University
www.alasu.edu

Auburn University
www.auburn.edu

Auburn
    University–Montgomery
www.aum.edu

Birmingham–Southern
    College
www.bsc.edu

Jacksonville State University
www.jsu.edu

Troy State University–Troy
www.troyst.edu

University of
    Alabama–Birmingham
www.uab.edu

University of Mobile
www.umobile.edu

University of South Alabama
www.southalabama.edu

Alaska

University of
    Alaska–Anchorage
www.uaa.alaska.edu

University of
    Alaska–Fairbanks
www.uaf.edu

Arizona

Grand Canyon University
www.grand-canyon.edu

Northern Arizona University
www.nau.edu

University of Arizona
www.arizona.edu

Arkansas

Arkansas State University
www.astate.edu

Harding University
www.harding.edu

Henderson State University
www.hsu.edu

Southern Arkansas University
www.saumag.edu

University of Arkansas, Main
  Campus
www.uark.edu

University of Central
  Arkansas
www.uca.edu

California

Armstrong University
www.armstrong-u.edu

Azusa Pacific University
www.apu.edu

California State
  University–Bakersfield
www.csub.edu

California State
  University–Dominguez
  Hills
www.csudh.edu

California State
  University–Fresno
www.csufresno.edu

California State
  University–Fullerton
www.fullerton.edu

California State
  University–Long Beach
www.csulb.edu

California State
  University–Los Angeles
www.calstatela.edu

California State
  University–Northridge
www.csun.edu

California State
  University–Sacramento
www.csus.edu

California State
  University–Stanislaus
www.csustan.edu

Golden Gate University
www.ggu.edu

La Sierra University
www.lasierra.edu

Notre Dame de Namur
   University
www.ndnu.edu

Pacific States University
www.psuca.edu

Pacific Union College
www.puc.edu

San Diego State University
www.sdsu.edu

San Francisco State University
www.sfsu.edu

Santa Clara University
www.scu.edu

University of La Verne
www.ulaverne.edu

University of the Pacific
www.uop.edu

University of San Francisco
www.usfca.edu

Colorado

Adams State University
www.adams.edu

Colorado Christian University
www.ccu.edu

University of
   Colorado–Colorado
   Springs
www.uccs.edu

University of Denver
www.du.edu

Connecticut

Central Connecticut State
   University
www.ccsu.edu

Fairfield University
www.fairfield.edu

Quinnipiac College
www.quinnipiac.edu

Southern Connecticut State
   University
www.southernct.edu

University of Bridgeport
www.bridgeport.edu

University of
   Connecticut–Storrs
www.uconn.edu

University of Hartford
www.hartford.edu

University of New Haven
www.newhaven.edu

Delaware

Delaware State University
www.dsc.edu

University of Delaware
www.udel.edu

Wesley College
www.wesley.edu

District of Columbia

American University
www.american.edu

Howard University
www.howard.edu

Mount Vernon College
www.mvc.gwu.edu

Southeastern University
www.seu.edu

University of the District of
Columbia
www.universityofdc.org

Florida

Barry University
www.barry.edu

Florida Institute of
Technology
www.fit.edu

Florida Metropolitan
University–Tampa
www.fmu.edu

Florida Southern College
www.flsouthern.edu

Florida State University
www.fsu.edu

Herzing College
www.herzing.edu/orlando

Jacksonville University
www.ju.edu

Lynn University
www.lynn.edu

Schiller International
University–Florida
www.schiller.edu

St. Thomas University
www.stu.edu

Stetson University
www.stetson.edu

University of Central Florida
www.ucf.edu

University of Miami
www.miami.edu

University of North Florida
www.unf.edu

University of South Florida
www.usf.edu

University of Tampa
www.utampa.edu

University of West Florida
www.uwf.edu

Georgia

Albany State College
http://asuweb.asurams.edu

Augusta State University
www.aug.edu

Emory University
www.emory.edu

Georgia College and State
University
www.gcsu.edu

Georgia Southern University
www.georgiasouthern.edu

Georgia Southwestern State
University
www.gsw.edu

Kennesaw College
www.kennesaw.edu

Mercer University–Atlanta
www.mercer.edu

North Georgia College
www.ngcsu.edu

University of Georgia
www.uga.edu

Valdosta State University
www.valdosta.edu

Hawaii

Chaminade University of
Honolulu
www.chaminade.edu

Hawaii Pacific University
www.hpu.edu

University of Hawaii–Manoa
www.hawaii.edu

Idaho

Boise State University
www.boisestate.edu

Idaho State University
www.isu.edu

University of Idaho
www.uidaho.edu

Illinois

Aurora University
www.aurora.edu

Benedictine University
www.ben.edu

Bradley University
www.bradley.edu

Chicago State University
www.csu.edu

College of Saint Francis
www.stfrancis.edu

Columbia College
www.colum.edu

DePaul University
www.depaul.edu

Illinois State University
www.ilstu.edu

Lewis University
www.lewisu.edu

Loyola University of Chicago
www.luc.edu

North Central College
www.noctrl.edu

North Park College
www.northpark.edu

Northeastern Illinois
University
www.neiu.edu

Northern Illinois University
www.niu.edu

Olivet Nazarene University
www.olivet.edu

Quincy College
www.quincycollege.edu

Southern Illinois
University–Carbondale
www.siuc.edu

University of Illinois at
Urbana–Champaign
www.uiuc.edu

Western Illinois University
www.wiu.edu

Indiana

Anderson University
www.anderson.edu

Ball State University
www.bsu.edu

Butler University
www.butler.edu

Indiana Institute of
Technology
www.indtech.edu

Indiana Wesleyan University
www.indwes.edu

Oakland City University
www.oak.edu

St. Mary-of-the-Woods
College
www.smwc.edu

University of Evansville
www.evansville.edu

University of Indianapolis
www.uindy.edu

University of Notre Dame
www.nd.edu

University of Southern
Indiana
www.usi.edu

Valparaiso University
www.valpo.edu

Iowa

Buena Vista University
www.bvu.edu

Clarke College
www.clarke.edu

Drake University
www.drake.edu

Iowa State University
www.iastate.edu

Loras College
www.loras.edu

University of Dubuque
www.dbq.edu

University of Iowa
www.uiowa.edu

University of Northern Iowa
www.uni.edu

Upper Iowa University
www.uiu.edu

Kansas

Emporia State University
www.emporia.edu

Fort Hays State University
www.fhsu.edu

Kansas Newman College
www.newmanu.edu

Kansas State University
www.ksu.edu

Pittsburg State University
www.pittstate.edu

Washburn University of
Topeka
www.washburn.edu

Wichita State University
www.wichita.edu

Kentucky

Eastern Kentucky University
www.eku.edu

Georgetown College
www.georgetowncollege.edu

Murray State University
www.murraystate.edu

Louisiana

Grambling State University
www.gram.edu

Louisiana State
University–Shreveport
www.lsus.edu

Loyola University
www.loyno.edu

Northeast Louisiana
University
www.ulm.edu

Southern University–Baton
Rouge
www.subr.edu

University of New Orleans
www.uno.edu

University of Southwestern
Louisiana
www.louisiana.edu

Xavier University of Louisiana
www.xula.edu

Maine

Husson College
www.husson.edu

Saint Joseph's College
www.sjcme.edu

Thomas College
www.thomas.edu

University of Maine at Orono
www.umaine.edu

Maryland

Loyola College
www.loyola.edu

Morgan State University
www.morgan.edu

University of Baltimore
www.ubalt.edu

University of
    Maryland–College Park
www.umd.edu

Massachusetts

American International
    College
www.aic.edu

Babson College
www.babson.edu

Boston College
www.bc.edu

Elms College
www.elms.edu

Nichols College
www.nichols.edu

Salem State College
www.salemstate.edu

Simmons College
www.simmons.edu

Suffolk University
www.suffolk.edu

University of
    Massachusetts–Amherst
www.umass.edu

University of
    Massachusetts–Dartmouth
www.umassd.edu

Western New England College
www.wnec.edu

Michigan

Andrews University
www.andrews.edu

Baker College
www.baker.edu

Central Michigan University
www.cmich.edu

Eastern Michigan University
www.emich.edu

Ferris State College
www.ferris.edu

Grand Valley State University
www.gvsu.edu

Madonna University
www.munet.edu

Michigan State University
www.msu.edu

Northern Michigan University
www.nmu.edu

Oakland University
www.oakland.edu

Wayne State University
www.wayne.edu

Western Michigan University
www.wmich.edu

Minnesota

Augsburg College
www.augsburg.edu

Bethel University
www.bethel.edu

College of St. Catherine
www.stkate.edu

Minnesota State
University–Moorhead
www.mnstate.edu

Southwest Minnesota State
University
www.southwest.msus.edu

St. Cloud State University
www.stcloudstate.edu

University of
Minnesota–Twin Cities
www.umn.edu

Winona State University
www.winona.edu

Mississippi

Delta State University
www.deltastate.edu

Jackson State University
www.jsums.edu

Mississippi State University
www.msstate.edu

University of Mississippi
www.olemiss.edu

University of Southern
Mississippi
www.usm.edu

Missouri

Avila College
www.avila.edu

Central Missouri State
University
www.cmsu.edu

Fontbonne College
www.fontbonne.edu

Lincoln University
www.lincolnu.edu

Northwest Missouri State
University
www.nwmissouri.edu

Rockhurst College
www.rockhurst.edu

Southeast Missouri State
University
www.semo.edu

Southwest Missouri State
University
www.smsu.edu

St. Louis University
www.slu.edu

Truman State University
www.truman.edu

Webster University
www.webster.edu

William Woods College
www.wmwoods.edu

Montana

Montana State
University–Billings
www.msubillings.edu

University of Great Falls
www.ugf.edu

University of Montana
www.umt.edu

Nebraska

Creighton University
www.creighton.edu

Hastings College
www.hastings.edu

Peru State College
www.peru.edu

Union College
www.ucollege.edu

University of
Nebraska–Omaha
www.unomaha.edu

Nevada

University of
Nevada–Las Vegas
www.unlv.edu

University of Nevada–Reno
www.unr.edu

New Hampshire

New Hampshire College
www.nhc.edu

Plymouth State College
www.plymouth.edu

Rivier College
www.rivier.edu

New Jersey

Fairleigh Dickinson University
www.fdu.edu

New Jersey City University
www.njcu.edu

St. Peter's College
www.spc.edu

Thomas Edison State College
www.tesc.edu

New Mexico

College of the Southwest
www.csw.edu

Eastern New Mexico
University
www.enmu.edu

New Mexico Highlands
University
www.nmhu.edu

New Mexico State University
www.nmsu.edu

University of New Mexico
www.unm.edu

Western New Mexico
University
www.wnmu.edu

New York

Canisius College
www.canisius.edu

City University of New York
www.cuny.edu

Clarkson University
www.clarkson.edu

CUNY-Bernard M. Baruch
College
www.baruch.cuny.edu

Dowling College
www.dowling.edu

Iona College
www.iona.edu

Ithaca College
www.ithaca.edu

Long Island
University–Brooklyn
Campus
www.liu.edu

Long Island
University–C. W. Post
Campus
www.cwpost.liu.edu

New York University
www.nyu.edu

Niagara University
www.niagara.edu

Pace University–New York
www.pace.edu

Pace University–Pleasantville
www.pace.edu

Parsons School of Design
www.parsons.edu

Saint John's University
www.stjohns.edu

Siena College
www.siena.edu

St. Bonaventure University
www.sbu.edu

St. Joseph's College
www.sjcny.edu

St. Thomas Aquinas College
www.stac.edu

State University of New York,
College at Oswego
www.oswego.edu

Syracuse University
www.syr.edu

Touro College
www.touro.edu

North Carolina

Appalachian State University
www.acs.appstate.edu

East Carolina University
www.ecu.edu

Fayetteville State University
www.uncfsu.edu

Pfeiffer College
www.pfeiffer.edu

University of North
Carolina–Greensboro
www.uncg.edu

University of North
Carolina–Wilmington
www.uncw.edu

Western Carolina University
www.wcu.edu

North Dakota

University of North
Dakota–Grand Forks
www.und.edu

Ohio

Ashland University
www.ashland.edu

Baldwin-Wallace College
www.bw.edu

Bowling Green State
University
www.bgsu.edu

Central State University
www.centralstate.edu

Defiance College
www.defiance.edu

Franciscan University of
Steubenville
www.franciscan.edu

John Carroll University
www.jcu.edu

Kent State University
www.kent.edu

Marietta College
www.marietta.edu

Miami University–Oxford
www.muohio.edu

Notre Dame College of Ohio
www.ndc.edu

Ohio State
University–Columbus
www.osu.edu

Ohio University–Athens
www.ohiou.edu

Otterbein College
www.otterbein.edu

University of Cincinnati
www.uc.edu

University of Dayton
www.udayton.edu

University of Findlay
www.findlay.edu

University of Rio Grande
www.urgrgcc.edu

University of Toledo
www.utoledo.edu

Walsh University
www.walsh.edu

Wright State University
www.wright.edu

Xavier University
www.xu.edu

Youngstown State University
www.ysu.edu

Oklahoma

East Central University
www.ecok.edu

Northeastern State University
www.nsuok.edu

Oklahoma Baptist University
www.okbu.edu

Oklahoma Christian College
www.oc.edu

Oklahoma City University
www.okcu.edu

Oral Roberts University
www.oru.edu

Southeastern Oklahoma State
University
www.sosu.edu

Southwestern Oklahoma State
University
www.swosu.edu

University of Central
Oklahoma
www.ucok.edu

University of Tulsa
www.utulsa.edu

Oregon

Northwest Christian College
www.nwcc.edu

Oregon State University
www.oregonstate.edu

Portland State University
www.pdx.edu

University of Portland
www.up.edu

Pennsylvania

Allentown College of Saint
Francis de Sales
www.desales.edu

Cabrini College
www.cabrini.edu

California University of
Pennsylvania
www.cup.edu

Carnegie Mellon University
www.cmu.edu

Clarion University of
Pennsylvania
www.clarion.edu

College of Misericordia
www.misericordia.edu

Drexel University
www.drexel.edu

Duquesne University
www.duq.edu

Edinboro University of
Pennsylvania
www.edinboro.edu

Gannon University
www.gannon.edu

Geneva College
www.geneva.edu

Grove City College
www.gcc.edu

Holy Family College
www.hfc.edu

Indiana University of
Pennsylvania
www.iup.edu

King's College
www.kings.edu

La Salle University
www.lasalle.edu

Marywood College
www.marywood.edu

Philadelphia University
www.philau.edu

Seton Hill College
www.setonhill.edu

Shippensburg University of
Pennsylvania
www.ship.edu

Slippery Rock University
www.sru.edu

St. Joseph's University
www.sju.edu

Temple University
www.temple.edu

University of Pennsylvania
www.upenn.edu

University of Scranton
www.scranton.edu

Villanova University
www.villanova.edu

Waynesburg College
www.waynesburg.edu

West Chester University of
Pennsylvania
www.wcupa.edu

York College of Pennsylvania
www.ycp.edu

Rhode Island

Bryant College
www.bryant.edu

Johnson & Wales University
www.jwu.edu

Providence College
www.providence.edu

Rhode Island College
www.ric.edu

University of Rhode Island
www.uri.edu

South Carolina

Bob Jones University
www.bju.edu

Charleston Southern
University
www.csuniv.edu

Clemson University
www.clemson.edu

South Carolina State College
www.scsu.edu

University of South Carolina
www.sc.edu

University of South
Carolina–Aiken
www.usca.edu

South Dakota

Dakota State University
www.dsu.edu

Northern State University
www.northern.edu

Tennessee

Austin Peay State University
www.apsu.edu

Belmont University
www.belmont.edu

Christian Brothers University
www.cbu.edu

Cumberland University
www.cumberland.edu

East Tennessee State
University
www.etsu.edu

Freed-Hardeman University
www.fhu.edu

Lincoln Memorial University
www.lmunet.edu

Middle Tennessee State
University
www.mtsu.edu

Southern Adventists
University
www.southern.edu

Tennessee Tech University
www.tntech.edu

Union University
www.uu.edu

University of Memphis
www.memphis.edu

University of
Tennessee Knoxville
www.utk.edu

University of
Tennessee–Martin
www.utm.edu

Texas

Abilene Christian University
www.acu.edu

Amberton University
www.amberton.edu

Angelo State University
www.angelo.edu

Baylor University
www.baylor.edu

Dallas Baptist University
www.dbu.edu

Hardin-Simmons University
www.hsutx.edu

Houston Baptist University
www.hbu.edu

Le Tourneau University
www.letu.edu

Midwestern State University
www.mwsu.edu

Prairie View A & M
University
www.pvamu.edu

Sam Houston State University
www.shsu.edu

Southwest Texas State
University
www.swt.edu

St. Mary's University
www.stmarytx.edu

Stephen F. Austin State
University
www.sfasu.edu

Tarleton State University
www.tarleton.edu

Texas A & M International
University
www.tamiu.edu

Texas A & M
University–Main Campus
www.tamu.edu

Texas A & M
University–Commerce
www.tamu-commerce.edu

Texas A & M
University–Kingsville
www.tamuk.edu

Texas Southern University
www.tsu.edu

Texas Tech University
www.ttu.edu

Texas Wesleyan University
www.txwes.edu

University of
Houston–Clear Lake
www.cl.uh.edu

University of
Houston–University Park
www.uh.edu

University of Incarnate Word
www.uiw.edu

University of North Texas
www.unt.edu

University of Texas–El Paso
www.utep.edu

University of
   Texas–Pan American
www.panam.edu

University of Texas of
   Permian Basin
www.utpb.edu

West Texas A & M University
www.wtamu.edu

Utah

Brigham Young University
www.byu.edu

University of Utah
www.utah.edu

Utah State University
www.usu.edu

Weber State University
www.weber.edu

Vermont

Castleton State College
www.csc.vsc.edu

Virginia

Averett College
www.averett.edu

Christopher Newport
   University
www.cnu.edu

Hampton University
www.hamptonu.edu

James Madison University
www.jmu.edu

Marymount University
www.marymount.edu

Old Dominion University
www.odu.edu

Radford University
www.radford.edu

Virginia Commonwealth
   University
www.vcu.edu

Virginia Tech University
www.vt.edu

Washington

Central Washington
University
www.cwu.edu

City University
www.cityu.edu

Eastern Washington
University
www.ewu.edu

Pacific Lutheran University
www.plu.edu

Seattle University
www.seattleu.edu

Walla Walla College
www.wwc.edu

Washington State University
www.wsu.edu

West Virginia

Marshall University
www.marshall.edu

Salem International University
www.salemiu.edu

University of Charleston
www.uchaswv.edu

West Virginia State College
www.wvsc.edu

West Virginia Wesleyan
College
www.wvwc.edu

Wheeling Jesuit College
www.wju.edu

Wisconsin

Carthage College
www.carthage.edu

Lakeland College
www.lakeland.edu

Marian College of Fond
du Lac
www.mariancoll.edu

Marquette University
www.marquette.edu

University of
Wisconsin–Eau Claire
www.uwec.edu

University of
Wisconsin–Madison
www.wisc.edu

University of
   Wisconsin–Milwaukee
www.uwm.edu

University of
   Wisconsin–Oshkosh
www.uwosh.edu

University of
   Wisconsin–Superior
www.uwsuper.edu

University of
   Wisconsin–Whitewater
www.uww.edu

Viterbo College
www.viterbo.edu

Doctoral Degree

The following schools offer doctoral degrees in both marketing and marketing-related subjects.

Alabama

Auburn University
www.auburn.edu

Auburn
   University–Montgomery
www.aum.edu

University of
   Alabama–Birmingham
www.uab.edu

University of South Alabama
www.southalabama.edu

Alaska

University of
   Alaska–Fairbanks
www.uaf.edu

Arizona

Northern Arizona University
www.nau.edu

University of Arizona
www.arizona.edu

Arkansas

Arkansas State University
www.astate.edu

University of Arkansas, Main
Campus
www.uark.edu

California

Azusa Pacific University
www.apu.edu

California State
University–Fresno
www.csufresno.edu

Golden Gate University
www.ggu.edu

La Sierra University
www.lasierra.edu

Pacific States University
www.psuca.edu

San Diego State University
www.sdsu.edu

Santa Clara University
www.scu.edu

University of La Verne
www.ulaverne.edu

University of the Pacific
www.uop.edu

Colorado

Colorado State University
www.colostate.edu

University of
Colorado–Colorado
Springs
www.uccs.edu

University of Denver
www.du.edu

Connecticut

Quinnipiac College
www.quinnipiac.edu

University of Bridgeport
www.bridgeport.edu

University of New Haven
www.newhaven.edu

Delaware

University of Delaware
www.udel.edu

District of Columbia

American University
www.american.edu

Howard University
www.howard.edu

Florida

Barry University
www.barry.edu

Florida Institute of
Technology
www.fit.edu

Florida State University
www.fsu.edu

St. Thomas University
www.stu.edu

Stetson University
www.stetson.edu

University of Central Florida
www.ucf.edu

University of Miami
www.miami.edu

University of North Florida
www.unf.edu

University of South Florida
www.usf.edu

Georgia

Emory University
www.emory.edu

Georgia Southern University
www.georgiasouthern.edu

Mercer University–Atlanta
www.mercer.edu

University of Georgia
www.uga.edu

Valdosta State University
www.valdosta.edu

Hawaii

University of Hawaii–Manoa
www.hawaii.edu

Idaho

Boise State University
www.boisestate.edu

Idaho State University
www.isu.edu

University of Idaho
www.uidaho.edu

Illinois

Benedictine University
www.ben.edu

DePaul University
www.depaul.edu

Illinois State University
www.ilstu.edu

Loyola University of Chicago
www.luc.edu

North Park University
www.northpark.edu

Northeastern Illinois
University
www.neiu.edu

Northern Illinois University
www.niu.edu

Southern Illinois
University–Carbondale
www.siuc.edu

University of Illinois at
Urbana–Champaign
www.uiuc.edu

Indiana

Anderson University
www.anderson.edu

Ball State University
www.bsu.edu

Indiana State University
www.indstate.edu

University of Indianapolis
www.uindy.edu

University of Notre Dame
www.nd.edu

Valparaiso University
www.valpo.edu

Iowa

Drake University
www.drake.edu

Iowa State University
www.iastate.edu

University of Dubuque
www.dbq.edu

University of Iowa
www.uiowa.edu

University of Northern Iowa
www.uni.edu

Kansas

Emporia State University
www.emporia.edu

Kansas State University
www.ksu.edu

Washburn University of
Topeka
www.washburn.edu

Wichita State University
www.wichita.edu

Louisiana

Grambling State University
www.gram.edu

Loyola University
www.loyno.edu

Northeast Louisiana
University
www.ulm.edu

Southern University–Baton
Rouge
www.subr.edu

University of New Orleans
www.uno.edu

University of Southwestern
Louisiana
www.louisiana.edu

Xavier University of Louisiana
www.xula.edu

Maine

University of Maine at Orono
www.umaine.edu

Maryland

Loyola College
www.loyola.edu

Morgan State University
www.morgan.edu

University of Baltimore
www.ubalt.edu

University of
Maryland–College Park
www.umd.edu

Massachusetts

American International
College
www.aic.edu

Simmons College
www.simmons.edu

Suffolk University
www.suffolk.edu

University of
Massachusetts–Amherst
www.umass.edu

University of
Massachusetts–Dartmouth
www.umassd.edu

Western New England College
www.wnec.edu

Michigan

Andrews University
www.andrews.edu

Central Michigan University
www.cmich.edu

Eastern Michigan University
www.emich.edu

Ferris State College
www.ferris.edu

Michigan State University
www.msu.edu

Oakland University
www.oakland.edu

Wayne State University
www.wayne.edu

Western Michigan University
www.wmich.edu

Minnesota

St. Cloud State University
www.stcloudstate.edu

University of
Minnesota–Twin Cities
www.umn.edu

Mississippi

Delta State University
www.deltastate.edu

Jackson State University
www.jsums.edu

Mississippi State University
www.msstate.edu

University of Mississippi
www.olemiss.edu

University of Southern
Mississippi
www.usm.edu

Missouri

St. Louis University
www.slu.edu

Webster University
www.webster.edu

Montana

University of Montana
www.umt.edu

Nebraska

Creighton University
www.creighton.edu

University of
Nebraska–Omaha
www.unomaha.edu

Nevada

University of
Nevada–Las Vegas
www.unlv.edu

University of Nevada–Reno
www.unr.edu

New Jersey

Farleigh Dickinson University
www.fdu.edu

New Mexico

New Mexico State University
www.nmsu.edu

University of New Mexico
www.unm.edu

New York

City University of New York
www.cuny.edu

CUNY-Bernard M. Baruch
College
www.baruch.cuny.edu

Long Island
University–Brooklyn
Campus
www.liu.edu

Long Island
University–C. W. Post
Campus
www.cwpost.liu.edu

New York University
www.nyu.edu

Pace University–New York
www.pace.edu

Pace University–Pleasantville
www.pace.edu

Rochester Institute of
Technology
www.rit.edu

Saint John's University
www.stjohns.edu

Syracuse University
www.syr.edu

Touro College
www.touro.edu

North Carolina

Appalachian State University
www.acs.appstate.edu

East Carolina University
www.ecu.edu

Fayetteville State University
www.uncfsu.edu

University of North
Carolina–Greensboro
www.uncg.edu

Western Carolina University
www.wcu.edu

North Dakota

University of North
Dakota–Grand Forks
www.und.edu

Ohio

Ashland University
www.ashland.edu

Bowling Green State
University
www.bgsu.edu

Kent State University
www.kent.edu

Miami University–Oxford
www.muohio.edu

Ohio State
University–Columbus
www.osu.edu

Ohio University–Athens
www.ohiou.edu

University of Cincinnati
www.uc.edu

University of Dayton
www.udayton.edu

University of Toledo
www.utoledo.edu

Wright State University
www.wright.edu

Xavier University
www.xu.edu

Youngstown State University
www.ysu.edu

Oklahoma

Northeastern State University
www.nsuok.edu

Oklahoma City University
www.okcu.edu

Oral Roberts University
www.oru.edu

University of Tulsa
www.utulsa.edu

Oregon

Oregon State University
www.oregonstate.edu

Portland State University
www.pdx.edu

Pennsylvania

Drexel University
www.drexel.edu

Duquesne University
www.duq.edu

Indiana University of
Pennsylvania
www.iup.edu

Marywood College
www.marywood.edu

Temple University
www.temple.edu

University of Pennsylvania
www.upenn.edu

Villanova University
www.villanova.edu

Rhode Island

Providence College
www.providence.edu

Rhode Island College
www.ric.edu

University of Rhode Island
www.uri.edu

South Carolina

Bob Jones University
www.bju.edu

Clemson University
www.clemson.edu

Limestone College
www.limestone.edu

South Carolina State
University
www.scsu.edu

University of South Carolina
www.sc.edu

Tennessee

East Tennessee State
University
www.etsu.edu

Middle Tennessee State
University
www.mtsu.edu

Tennessee Tech University
www.tntech.edu

University of Memphis
www.memphis.edu

University of
Tennessee–Knoxville
www.utk.edu

Texas

Abilene Christian University
www.acu.edu

Baylor University
www.baylor.edu

Hardin-Simmons University
www.hsutx.edu

Sam Houston State University
www.shsu.edu

Southwest Texas State
University
www.swt.edu

Stephen F. Austin State
University
www.sfasu.edu

Tarleton State University
www.tarleton.edu

Texas A & M
University–Main Campus
www.tamu.edu

Texas A & M
University–Commerce
www.tamu-commerce.edu

Texas A & M
University–Kingsville
www.tamuk.edu

Texas Southern University
www.tsu.edu

Texas Tech University
www.ttu.edu

Texas Wesleyan University
www.txwes.edu

University of
Houston–Clear Lake
www.cl.uh.edu

University of
Houston–University Park
www.uh.edu

University of North Texas
www.unt.edu

University of Texas–El Paso
www.utep.edu

University of
Texas–San Antonio
www.utsa.edu

Utah

Brigham Young University
www.byu.edu

University of Utah
www.utah.edu

Utah State University
www.usu.edu

Virginia

Hampton University
www.hamptonu.edu

James Madison University
www.jmu.edu

Old Dominion University
www.odu.edu

Virginia Commonwealth
University
www.vcu.edu

Virginia Tech University
www.vt.edu

Washington

Seattle University
www.seattleu.edu

Washington State University
www.wsu.edu

West Virginia

Marshall University
www.marshall.edu

Wisconsin

Marquette University
www.marquette.edu

University of
Wisconsin–Madison
www.wisc.edu

University of
Wisconsin–Milwaukee
www.uwm.edu

Appendix B

Professional Organizations

The following is a list of associations with professional members in various facets of marketing and related areas. For further information, you may contact the organization directly either by phone or by mail. Most groups welcome inquiries, and some even accept student members. You will notice some industry-specific associations. We have included only a representative group, but you may research any industry of particular interest by consulting the *Encyclopedia of Associations,* which also gives a thumbnail sketch of the aims of the organizations.

Of special interest to marketers in general is the American Marketing Association (AMA), the organization for marketing professionals. The AMA has collegiate, local, and national chapters dedicated to furthering the practice of marketing and to educating the public in the ethical conduct of business.

The *Encyclopedia of Associations,* published by Gale Research Company and available in the reference section of most libraries, is a valuable source of information on professional and trade associations. Each entry lists the address of the organization and the name of the current director. It also provides some background information on the group and its focus. Some general categories to check in this publication are: advertising, public relations, communications, marketing, sales, retailing, product management, or any industry of special interest to you.

Academy of Marketing Science
School of Business Administration
University of Miami
P.O. Box 248012
Coral Gables, FL 33124-6536
www.ams-web.org/index.cfm

Advertising Club of New York
235 Park Ave. South, 6th Fl.
New York, NY 10003-1450
www.theadvertisingclub.org

The Advertising Council, Inc.
261 Madison Ave., 11th Fl.
New York, NY 10016
www.adcouncil.org/orgs/the_advertising_council_inc

Advertising Research Foundation
(Association of National Advertisers)
641 Lexington Ave.
New York, NY 10022
www.arfsite.org

Advertising Women of New York
25 W. 45th St., Ste. 1001
New York, NY 10036
www.awny.org

Affiliated Advertising Agencies International
2280 S. Xanadu Way, Ste. 300
Aurora, CO 80014

American Advertising Federation
1101 Vermont Ave. NW, Ste. 500
Washington, DC 20005-6306
www.aaf.org

American Association of Advertising Agencies, Inc.
405 Lexington Ave., 18th Fl.
New York, NY 10174-1801
www.aaaa.org

American Marketing Association
311 S. Wacker Dr., Ste. 5800
Chicago, IL 60606
www.ama.org
www.marketingpower.com

American Telemarketing Association
(American Teleservices Association)
3815 River Crossing Pkwy., Ste. 20
Indianapolis, IN 46240
www.ataconnect.org

Association of Free Community Papers (AFCP)
1630 Miner St., Ste. 204
Box 1989
Idaho Springs, CO 80452
www.afcp.org

Association of Incentive Marketing (AIM)
244 Broad St.
Red Bank, NJ 07701-2003
www.aim-online.org

Association for Women in Communications
780 Ritchie Hwy., Ste. 28S
Severna Park, MD 21146
www.womcom.org

Automotive Communication Council
(Automotive Advertisers Council)
4600 East West Highway
Bethesda, MD 20814
www.acc-online.org

Bank Marketing Association
(American Bankers Association)
1120 Connecticut Ave. NW
Washington, DC 20036
www.aba.com

Biomedical Marketing Association
10293 N. Meridian St., Ste. 175
Indianapolis, IN 46290
www.bmaonline.org

Business Marketing Association
(Business/Professional Advertising Association)
400 N. Michigan Ave., 15th Fl.
Chicago, IL 60611
www.marketing.org

Crain Communications Inc., Human Resources
711 Third Ave.
New York, NY 10017-4036
www.crain.com

Direct Marketing Association
1120 Avenue of the Americas
New York, NY 10036-6700
www.the-dma.org

Direct Selling Association
1275 Pennsylvania Ave. NW, Ste. 800
Washington, DC 20004
www.dsa.org

Institute of Outdoor Advertising
(Outdoor Advertising Association of America)
1850 M St. NW, Ste. 1040
Washington, DC 20036
www.oaaa.org

The Institute for Public Relations
P.O. Box 118400
2096 Weimer Hall
Gainesville, FL 32611-8400
www.instituteforpr.com

Intermarket Association of Advertising Agencies
(Interactive Affiliate Network)
1605 N. Main St.
Dayton, OH 45405
www.ian.com

International Advertising Association
World Secretariat
521 Fifth Ave., Ste. 1807
New York, NY 10175
www.iaaglobal.org

International Association of Business Communicators
IABC World Headquarters Staff
1 Hallidie Plaza, Ste. 600
San Francisco, CA 94102
www.iabc.com/homepage.htm

International Federation of Advertising Agencies
1450 E. American La., Ste. 1400
Schaumburg, IL 60173-4973

International Marketing Institute
314 Hammond St., Ste. 52
Chestnut Hill, MA 02167-1206
www.smei.org

International Mass Retail Association
(Retail Industry Leaders Association)
1700 N. Moore St., Ste. 2250
Arlington, VA 22209
www.retail-leaders.org

International Public Relations Association
1, Dunley Hill Court
Ranmore Common
Dorking
Surrey, RH5 6SX
United Kingdom
www.ipra.org

Life Communicators Association
(Insurance and Finance Communicators Association)
P.O. Box 387
East Rutherford, NJ 07073
www.ifcaonline.org

Mail Advertising Service Association
1421 Prince St., Ste. 410
Alexandria, VA 22314-2806
www.masa.org

Marketing Research Association
1344 Silas Deane Hwy., Ste. 306
Rocky Hill, CT 06067-1342
www.mra-net.org

Marketing Science Institute
1000 Massachusetts Ave.
Cambridge, MA 02138-5396
www.msi.org

Mutual Advertising Agency Network
25700 Science Park Dr., Ste. 200
Cleveland, OH 44122
www.maanet.com

National Advertising Review Board
(National Advertising Review Council)
70 W. Thirty-Sixth St., 13th Fl.
New York, NY 10018
www.narcpartners.org/aboutnarb.asp

National Association of Market Developers, Inc. (NAMD)
(National Alliance of Market Developers)
Niles Communication
29 E. Thirty-First St., 6th Fl.
New York, NY 10016
www.namdntl.org

National Association of Media Women
1185 Niskey Lake Rd. SW
Atlanta, GA 30331

National Association of Professional Saleswomen
5520 Cherokee Ave., Ste. 200
Alexandria, VA 22312

National Association of Publishers' Representatives
25224 Brucefield Rd.
Cleveland, OH 44122
www.naprassoc.com

National Association of Sales Professionals
11000 N. 130th Pl.
Scottsdale, AZ 85259
www.nasp.com

National Association of Women Business Owners
8405 Greensboro Dr., Ste. 800
McLean, VA 22102
www.nawbo.org

National Mail Order Association
2807 Polk St. NE
Minneapolis, MN 55418-2954
www.nmoa.org

National Retail Federation (NRF)
325 Seventh St. NW, Ste. 1000
Washington, DC 20004
www.nrf.com

National Society of Sales Training Executives
(Professional Society for Sales and Marketing Training)
180 N. LaSalle St., Ste. 1822
Chicago, IL 60601
www.smt.org

The Networking Institute, Inc.
505 Waltham St.
West Newton, MA 02465
www.virtualteams.com

Newspaper Advertising Bureau, Inc.
(Newspaper Association of America)
1921 Gallows Rd., Ste. 600
Vienna, VA 22182-3900
www.naa.org

Outdoor Advertising Association of America
Headquarters
1850 M St. NW, Ste. 1040
Washington, DC 20036
www.oaaa.org

Point-of-Purchase Advertising Institute (POPAI)
1660 L St. NW, 10th Fl.
Washington, DC 20036
www.popai.com

Promotion Marketing Association of America
(Promotion Marketing Association Inc.)
257 Park Ave. South, 1lth Fl., Ste. 1102
New York, NY 10010
www.pmalink.org

Public Relations Society of America
33 Maiden La., 11th Fl.
New York, NY 10038-5150
www.prsa.org

Public Relations Student Society of America
33 Maiden La., 11th Fl.
New York, NY 10038-5150
www.prssa.org

Publishers Marketing Association
627 Aviation Way
Manhattan Beach, CA 90266
www.pma-online.org

Radio Advertising Bureau, Inc.
1320 Greenway Dr., # 500
Irving, TX 75038
www.rab.com

Sales and Marketing Executives International
P.O. Box 1390
Sumas, WA 98295-1390
www.smei.org

Society for Marketing Professional Services
99 Canal Centre Plaza, Ste. 330
Alexandria, VA 22314
www.smps.org

Specialty Advertising Association International
(Promotional Products Association International)
3125 Skyway Circle North
Irving, TX 75038-3526
www.ppai.org

Technical Marketing Society of America
4383 Via Majorca
Cypress, CA 90680

Women in Advertising and Marketing
(The Association of Women in Communication)
780 Ritchie Hwy., Ste. 28S
Severna Park, MD 21146
www.womcom.org

Women in Direct Marketing International
224 Seventh St.
Garden City, NY 11530
www.wdmi.org

Women Executives in Public Relations
FDR Station , P.O. Box 7657
New York, NY 10150-7657
www.wepr.org

Women in Sales Association
8 Madison Ave.
P.O. Box M
Valhalla, NY 10595

Recommended Reading

Basye, Anne, and Jim Kobs. *Opportunities in Direct Marketing Careers.* Lincolnwood, Ill.: NTC Publishing, Inc., 1993.

Cafftey, Ed. *So You Want to Be in Advertising: A Guide to Success in a Fast-Paced Business.* New York: Arco Publishing Co., 1988.

Cochran, Chuck, and Donna Peerce. *Wow! Résumés for Sales and Marketing Careers.* New York: McGraw-Hill, 1998.

Cosgrove, Holli. *Encyclopedia of Careers and Vocational Guidance.* Chicago: J. G. Ferguson Publishing Co., 2002.

Hird, Caroline. *Careers in Marketing, Advertising and Public Relations.* Dover, N.H.: Kogan Page Ltd., 2003.

Mogel, Leonard. *Opportunities in Newspapers, Magazines, Books, Television, Radio, the Movies.* Old Saybrook, Conn.: Globe Pequot Press, Inc., 1988.

Norback, Craig T. *VGM's Careers Encyclopedia.* Lincolnwood, Ill.: NTC/Contemporary Publishing Group, Inc., 2001.

Occupational Outlook Handbook, 2004–5 edition. U.S. Government Printing Office.

Pattis, S. William. *Careers in Advertising*. Chicago: McGraw-Hill, 2004.

Rotman, Morris B. *Opportunities in Public Relations Careers*. Lincolnwood, Ill.: NTC/Contemporary Publishing Group, Inc., 2001.

In addition, you may want to check out some of the trade publications available in your library, such as:

Advertising Age
Adweek
Marketing and Media Decisions
Marketing News
Public Relations News
Sales and Marketing Management
Stores Magazine

About the Author

Margery Steinberg received her Ph.D. from the University of Connecticut and is currently a full-time faculty member in the management/marketing department at the University of Hartford, where she teaches marketing, retailing, and consumer behavior. Dr. Steinberg actively applies her marketing expertise to assist local not-for-profit organizations and she currently serves on several arts-related boards of directors. She is a strong proponent of service learning and has created the acclaimed Micro Business Incubator Program, which matches students with small business owners to assist in the revitalization of their businesses and their neighborhood. Steinberg also lends her knowledge and experience to local and national organizations as a consultant.